Mastering Prolog

Mastering Prolog

Robert J. Lucas

Includes Prolog for PC (DOS and Windows 3.1/95)

First published in 1996 by UCL Press

UCL Press Limited
University College London
Gower Street
London WC1E 6BT

and

1900 Frost Road, Suite 101
Bristol
Pennsylvania 19007-1598

The name of University College London (UCL) is a registered trade mark
used by UCL Press with the consent of the owner.

British Library Cataloguing-in-Publication Data
A CIP catalogue record for this book is available from the British Library.

Library of Congress Cataloging-in-Publication Data are available

ISBN:
1-85728-400-3 PB

Typeset in Palatino, Univers and Courier.
Printed and bound by
Biddles Ltd, Guildford and King's Lynn, England.

Contents

Preface

Keylink Prolog is an interpreted system written with the first-time user and educational user in mind. It conforms to Edinburgh syntax, which makes it suitable for use with a wide range of texts. On the IBM-compatible PC under DOS it has a very straightforward command line interface. Also available for IBM-compatibles is a Windows 3.1 version that is fully integrated into the Microsoft Windows environment. On an Archimedes it is a proper desktop application. Keylink Prolog allows the use of any editor already available on the PC or Archimedes. It will also run on the RM Nimbus.

It is hoped that this book will be of use to anyone learning Prolog for the first time, whether this is specifically a Prolog course or an AI course using Prolog. In particular, the contents can be used as teaching material for those parts of the Scottish Highers' knowledge-based systems course concerned with knowledge processing in Prolog. This book goes beyond what is required in the syllabus, which would take the reader to near the end of Chapter 6 (up to the simpler parts of list processing).

If you are a complete beginner at Prolog then try to learn each concept completely before moving on. It is far too easy to think that you understand a concept only to find yourself coming unstuck on that very concept much later, when it has now become muddled with additional material. Skipping a concept you find difficult will prove to be very costly at later stages. Prolog is built from a relatively small number of key features that interact in quite subtle ways. You need to be quite confident of the material covered before moving forward, so take your time. If you get completely stuck, try having a complete break from the machine and give yourself some time to digest what you have learnt. Do not worry if you find you need to read the same section many times. As with many subjects, practice at solving problems is the key to understanding. So do try the exercises; solutions to many of them are supplied at the end of the book.

This book includes a single-user licence for Keylink Prolog for the PC (DOS or Windows 3.1). If you want to run Keylink Prolog on a network then you must either obtain a network licence from Keylink or buy sufficient copies of the book to ensure that you have at least one licence per user. A RiscOS version is available for the Archimedes. A single-user licence can be obtained from Keylink Computers at a cost of £10 plus VAT.

Rob Lucas
Kenilworth, Warwickshire
August 1995

Keylink Prolog for RiscOS machines can be obtained from:

Keylink Computers Limited
2 Woodway House
Common Lane
Kenilworth
Warwickshire
CV8 2ES

Tel: 01926 850909
Fax: 01926 864128

Acknowledgements

Keylink Prolog has been used many times in teachers' in-service courses on Prolog. Jim Buchan of Northern College is to be thanked for his extensive "road testing" of the Prolog system and for giving it his endorsement. This book has been developed over many years of teaching Prolog and has recently been revised to reflect the requirements of school teaching in co-operation with Donny MacDonald of Forres Academy, Elgin.

James Hunter of King's College, Aberdeen, is to be thanked for allowing me to use some of his expert system class examples, which are in the MIKE chapter. They remain his copyright. Marc Eisenstadt and the Open University are to be thanked for allowing the MIKE expert system to be shipped with the Prolog package and also for allowing part of their code to be reproduced here. This material is copyright of the Open University and their permission and copyright notice as given in the file `mike.pl` should be noted.

More recently the text has been revised with a view to the requirements of university-level students, and Richard Gatward of Coventry University is to be thanked for his contribution, as are many of his students for pointing out errors and omissions over the past few years. Any further suggestions for improvements will be gratefully received. Many thanks are also due to Andrew Carrick of UCL Press for his many useful suggestions.

CHAPTER ONE

Introduction to Prolog

1.1 Background

Prolog is a logic-based computer language that allows a programmer to define rules and facts and to ask questions, more commonly called queries, about these. In English, facts are statements such as "The sky is grey" or "The wind is from the west". Rules are statements such as "I go shopping if the weather is fine and it is Saturday" or "It will rain if the sky is grey and the wind is from the west". A rule is characterized by "if", or its equivalent, connecting some conclusion with one or more premises. In the English statement of a rule, the word "if" might well be replaced by "when", as in "It will rain when the sky is grey and the wind is from the west", but from a logical point of view the use of "if" and "when" in such statements is equivalent.

The fact that Prolog deals with logic in a fairly direct way that allows us to store and use facts and rules makes it highly suitable as a knowledge representation language. Although it is possible to store knowledge in any computer language, it is the direct ability to store and use rules and facts that makes Prolog particularly useful.

When we ask Prolog a query, such as the Prolog equivalent of the English question "Will it rain?", Prolog will use the facts and rules in its database to try to construct a proof that it will rain, and it will report whether or not it was successful. It will construct a proof by demonstrating that the query can be logically deduced from the rules and facts.

In this example Prolog starts with the query "Will it rain?" and uses the rule "It will rain when the sky is grey and the wind is from the west" to establish that it must satisfy, or know to be true, the two separate statements "The sky is grey" and "The wind is from the west". If these two facts do exist for the Prolog system, i.e. it has been told them, then the query is satisfied and the Prolog system will report this. Here is how such a rule and the required facts may be expressed in Prolog; for the moment resist the temptation to type this into Prolog as you need to know a little bit more about using Prolog to make it run:

```
rain:-
    wind_is_westerly,
    sky_is_grey.
wind_is_westerly.
sky_is_grey.
```

The first three lines constitute the rule, while the final two are the facts. Given that :- is the Prolog equivalent to "if", and that the comma , represents "and", the rule may be read in a way that corresponds very closely to the English rule "Rain if wind is westerly and sky is grey". Similarly, the facts may be read as: wind is westerly and sky is grey. If we were to enter this rule and the two facts into Prolog's database and ask the query ?- rain, i.e. "Will it rain?", Prolog would reply yes.

Of course, there is a great deal more to Prolog than this, but this simple method of logical deduction is very much at the heart of Prolog and is the only method by which anything, trivial or otherwise, can be achieved.

The particular kind of logic used is a restricted first-order logic. Zero-order logic is the propositional calculus, which simply allows us to assign true or false to statements and combine statements in particularly inflexible ways to make deductions. This is a very restricted form of logic because we have no means of generalizing our knowledge to apply it to groups sharing the same properties. The example given above concerning whether it will rain is from zero-order logic. Statements such as "All men are mortal" cannot be usefully expressed in zero-order logic. First-order logic, also called predicate calculus, provides the necessary extensions to express and use statements of this type. The main problem with creating a computer program to execute first-order logic was that a very simple proof tended to need vast amounts of memory because it seemed necessary to generate and test a vast number of cases that were basically caused by the more general nature of the statements. The statement "All men are mortal" seems to imply that we need to be able to examine the entire domain of men. It was only as recently as 1965 that it was discovered how to keep the "proof trees" down to a manageable size (Robinson 1965). From then it was simply a matter of time before someone produced a computer implementation that could construct proofs in first-order logic. The first implementation appeared in 1972, developed at Marseilles University (Colmerauer 1973), and other implementations rapidly followed. In particular, Edinburgh University implemented DEC 10 Prolog, which has become accepted as a standard for Prolog syntax.

There are many books that treat the subject of logic from the point of view of using computers to prove theories in logic, such as Chang & Lee

(1973). This is a rather advanced text and is only likely to appeal to a mathematical audience. Formal logic as it applies to computing is covered in Dowsing (1986) and Boolos & Jeffrey (1974). A book that shows the connection between Prolog and the theory of logic is Gray (1984). This has the added advantage of also dealing with databases from a logical perspective. Another book that deals with Prolog and database applications is my own (Lucas 1988). While on the subject of books, another worth mentioning is *The craft of Prolog* (O'Keefe 1990), which is possibly the best of the advanced texts. It contains much useful information concerning efficiency issues and program style. It is one of the few texts that considers the issue of how Prolog executes as relevant to the Prolog programmer. To a lesser extent this is also true of *Prolog, a logical approach* (Dodd 1990). The earliest Prolog text is *Programming in Prolog* (Clocksin & Mellish 1981), often referred to simply as "Clocksin and Mellish". This is mentioned as it is referred to by almost everyone and, to some extent, helped to define a Prolog standard.

1.2 Interpreters and compilers

There are two sorts of Prolog system: Prolog interpreters and Prolog compilers. An interpreter (for any language, not just Prolog) stores a program in a form very much like the original text that has been typed in and translates it into the necessary instructions every time it needs to. A compiler, however, translates all the source code into the necessary machine code instructions only once. This allows the code to be executed immediately without the interpretation stage. Interpreters are popular because they are relatively easy to implement and offer programmers an interactive environment but, because of the repeated translation of the code that is necessary, they are much slower than compilers. In fact, most Prolog systems are a hybrid of interpreter and compiler, often called incremental compilers. These retain the interactiveness of an interpreter but offer increased performance as a result of partial compilation to an intermediate code, which can then be interpreted very much faster than the original source code. Compiling Prolog is a fascinating subject, and if you are interested in the techniques used then try reading Ait-Kaci (1991) and Dobry (1990). A general Prolog book that contains a good introduction to compilation techniques is Maier & Warren (1988). A book that I particularly recommend is *The architecture of symbolic computers* (Kogge 1991), which applies to other symbolic languages and is highly readable.

Keylink Prolog is a pure interpreter, but for the kind of programs that you will write any loss of performance when compared with a compiler version is of no significance.

1.3 What is a Prolog program?

A Prolog program consists of a series of facts and rules, expressed in the syntax of Prolog, which you input into the system's internal database. The rules are equivalent to procedures or subroutines in a conventional language, while the facts are equivalent to data items or data records.

You can query your database, that is you can ask questions about what facts are in the database. The rules define relationships between the facts and the rules themselves, and these relationships will be used by the Prolog system to answer the query. Asking a query is equivalent to running a program and, just as many subroutines or procedures may be invoked by running a program, so many rules may be brought into play by a query. Relevant rules are selected by a pattern matching process called unification. Making deductions from the rules and facts is the Prolog system's main job. These deductions are sometimes called inferences, because new facts are inferred from old rules and facts. The part of Prolog that does this is its inference engine. Because you specify only the data items and the relationships between rules and facts, Prolog is called non-procedural, that is you do not specify any algorithm to solve the problem but only relationships: the Prolog system uses the facts and rules to determine the algorithm at run time. There is a procedural side to Prolog, which amounts to understanding the procedural execution of the rules and facts by the Prolog system. In particular, this involves a knowledge of the order in which rules are executed, as this can be crucial.

The following diagram summarizes the Prolog system. A database stores the rules and facts that make up Prolog's current program. We enter a query and Prolog's inference engine tries to satisfy the query by trying to deduce it from the known rules and facts. Finally it returns one or more answers.

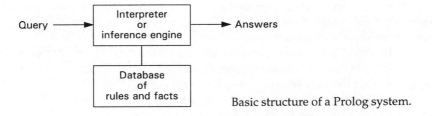

Basic structure of a Prolog system.

1.4 An initial session with Prolog

When it comes to actually using Prolog it is not important to have an intimate knowledge of logic. So if some of the above seems baffling do not worry: a few examples should clarify the main issues. There are a few things that you really have to get right, and in order to bring attention to these points there are paragraphs that are highlighted by being enclosed by horizontal lines. You should pay especial attention to these sections as ignoring them may cause you considerable grief.

To start the Keylink Prolog system on a PC under DOS type **prolog** followed by <Enter>. To start the Windows version, you should double click on the Prolog **?-** icon. To start Kprolog on an Archimedes double click on the **!Kprolog** icon.

The Prolog system will respond with a message giving the version number of the system and is now ready for you to input your facts, rules and queries. We will start with a simple query. All queries start with **?-**, and upon entry to Prolog this prompt is supplied. We terminate our input with a full-stop and return.

Everything we enter into the Prolog system must be terminated with a full-stop. If you forget to type it before pressing return you can do so it after the return and press return again. The first return in that case is treated as white space and is ignored.

In the following examples I will always show the **?-**, even though you do not need to type it. For your very first query type, remember that you do not need to type **?-**:

    ?- human.

human is the goal of this query – it is what the interpreter will try to prove. Prolog will simply answer **no** to this query because there is no entry in its internal database for **human,** or, to put it another way, the Prolog system was not able to prove the goal **human.**

Note on syntax errors

If you make a mistake before pressing return use the rub-out or backspace key to correct it. If there is a syntax error in a line you have input you will get an error message that will attempt to indicate the position of the error. However, Prolog needs the full-stop to tell it where the end of the sentence, or query, is. If, after inputting a query to which you expect a response, there is no response forthcoming then you may have missed out the full-stop. Simply type a full-stop and then press <Enter>.

If we want to input a fact into Prolog's database we need to ask the system to consult us, the user, for the fact or facts. To do this we type:

    ?- consult(user).

consult is a built-in function that can be used to load Prolog source code by giving it a file name or to allow us to input facts and rules directly into Prolog's database by using the pseudo file name "user".

Input this query and notice that the **?-** prompt has been replaced by a **|:** prompt, which indicates that Prolog is awaiting input other than a query. Now type (do not type the prompt!):

    |: human.

(Do not forget the full-stop.) This has entered the single fact **human.** straight into Prolog's database.

To return to what is called the *top-level interpreter*, where we get the **?-** prompt type:

    ?- seen.

Note that this time you do need to type **?-**. (This is a rather pedestrian way of inputting a fact and we will soon be using a much easier method.)

If you do not use **?- seen.** after **?- consult(user).** you will be stuck in the consult user mode, which you will probably find very frustrating as Prolog will not be trying to execute your queries. You may also forget to type the full-stop, which will have a similar result in that Prolog will not attempt to process your input until it sees a full-stop.

We can now repeat the previous query:

    ?- human.

The response will now be **yes**. The Prolog system replies either **yes** or **no** to any question we ask of it, so **yes** can be thought of as success or as an affirmation of what was queried, while **no** means failure. In this case, our query was satisfied trivially by the existence of the fact **human** in the database. More usually there would be some deduction involved – this we will meet soon.

Upon success, Prolog will not say **yes** if there are values of *variables* to report from the top-level query. **human** is a *constant*, sometimes called an *atom*, because it is an entity that cannot be split into smaller components. Non-numeric constants in Prolog always start with a lower-case letter, which can be followed by up to some large number of other alphanumeric or underscore characters. Anything beginning with an upper-case letter is treated as a variable by Prolog. We are about to come across examples of this. Now enter the query:

    ?- listing.

and the following should appear:

    human.

    yes

listing is recognized as a built-in command whose purpose is to list the current contents of the database. The entries in the database may be listed in a different form from that in which they were entered: some spaces may be added or removed to make the output appear neater. If you are unsure about the state of your database then **?- listing.** should clarify it. It is also possible when using the Windows version to list the contents of the database by choosing the menu item "Run" followed by "List Prolog Clauses". With the Archimedes, choosing "Listing" from the main menu has an identical effect.

There are many built-in commands, also called built-in predicates or BIPs, which will be explained as we come across them.

All built-in commands expect a given number of arguments, or parameters, which should be of a given type. Where a mistake is made in the number or type of an argument, Keylink Prolog will raise an exception, i.e. a message will be displayed indicating the type of the error, the command (goal) in which it occurred and the argument in question. For example:

```
?- listing(X).
!! Type error in argument 1
!! Goal is: listing(_32660)
!! atom expected
!! Execution aborted
```

The output of such errors can be turned on and off, and the status examined, by use of the built-in command **exceptions**, which is explained in Chapter 14. You should pay great attention to any exceptions that Prolog raises to your programs as they will help you make the necessary corrections.

Simple facts such as **human** are not of much use. In Prolog we can express relations between objects in the following form:

```
falcon(kestrel).
```

which we may take to mean "A kestrel is a falcon". Enter this fact into the internal database in the same way as **human.** was entered, i.e. type **?- consult(user).** Enter the fact (be careful to terminate with a full-stop and <Enter>) and then type **?- seen.** Type **?- listing.** to establish that you have entered the fact correctly and, if you have, make the following query:

```
?- falcon(X).
```

Note that X is an upper-case letter. As stated above, all variables in Prolog start with an upper-case letter, and may be followed by any combination of alphanumeric characters up to some arbitrary maximum length (255), and they may also contain underscore characters. This query may be read simply as "What X is a falcon?", and Prolog will reply with:

```
X = kestrel
```

7

The query has been successful *because a variable is allowed to stand for any constant* , and in this case X stands for kestrel. We say that X has become *instantiated* to kestrel. The matching process by which X becomes instantiated to kestrel is called *unification*.

We call **falcon(X)** the goal of the query. The top-level interpreter automatically tells us what the variable has become instantiated to in order to solve the query. It shows us these "top-level" instantiations as a convenience. We nearly always want to see these values and it saves us having to ask for them to be written.

To get back to the **?-** prompt on a PC, press <Return>. In the Windows version, when you are prompted **Another solution**, click on **No**. Select **Finish Query** on the Archimedes.

Another way to describe what has happened here is that the goal **falcon(X)** has been matched against the database entry **falcon(kestrel)**. Thus the goal has succeeded, causing X to be matched to kestrel. We can describe this with a diagram called a *solution tree*. This is a diagram that illustrates how the solution was arrived at. For such a simple example it does not tell us much, but it becomes more useful with more complicated examples:

```
?- falcon(X).
    |          {X = kestrel}
falcon(kestrel)
```

The solution tree starts with the query; we then indicate what is matched against the goals of the query (there is only one goal in this query). Here the vertical line joins the goal to the fact that it is matched against and any variable instantiations are indicated inside the curly brackets. Solution trees for many more examples, demonstrating their usefulness rather more clearly, are to be found later in the book.

Normally we need to make the Prolog system tell us what values variables have by using the **write** predicate, which is another built-in function like **listing**. Predicate means something that may or may not be true or proved, and is just logic's word for describing a goal.

Enter this query to see the effect of using write:

```
?- falcon(X), write(X).
```

However, when a variable occurs in our query, as in **?- falcon(X)**, the top-level interpreter will always show its value for a satisfied query. This may seem confusing, but in practice it adds to ease of use as it saves us having to type **write** over and over again. In the previous query the **,** stands for "and" so the query is "find an X such that falcon(X) is true (or exists) *and* then write the value of X".

In this case the query consists of two subgoals, **falcon(X)** and **write(X)**.

Now we are going to make another entry in the database that would satisfy this query. Enter the following fact into the internal database by using `?- consult(user).`:

    `falcon(peregrine).`

then, to return to the `?-` prompt, type:

    `?- seen.`

followed by the query:

    `?- listing.`

which will show you the updated database. Then enter the query:

    `?- falcon(X).`

For the moment, *do not* make any further input when you get the `X = kestrel` response.

The response is as before: adding the new fact has had no effect. This is because we have only actually asked for one solution and Prolog has given us the first one it found. Entering the query twice is also of no use in getting us the second entry, peregrine, because *for every query Prolog will start the search for a match from the start of the database.*

However, the top-level interpreter will allow us to get as many solutions for a particular query as we desire (as long as there are at least this number!) by inputting `;` (semicolon) after the first or subsequent solutions on the PC, or by selecting `Yes` to the `Another solution` prompt for the Windows version and `Next Solution` on the Archimedes. This is what the Windows prompt looks like:

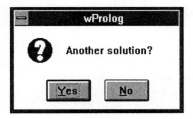

If there is another solution it will tell us what the necessary instantiation(s) were; if there are no more solutions it will give the response **no**. Type `;` or select `Yes/Next Solution` and you will immediately get the next solution. Type `;` again or select `Yes/Next Solution` again and the response will be **no**.

1.5 Failure

Another way to get both solutions is to make the query *fail* once it has found (and written) kestrel. This will force it to try and satisfy the query in a different way. The idea of failure is a very important one in Prolog: we met it above when our very first query **?- human.** failed because there was no matching fact in the database. What happens when a goal fails in Prolog is that it always tries to find an alternative way to satisfy (prove) the goal, by looking for alternative matches in the database. It always searches the database in order, using the first entry first and so on.

The only different way possible to solve the goal in our falcon example is to undo the instantiation of X to kestrel and continue searching the database for another match with the query goal. Type:

```
?- falcon(X), write(X), nl, fail.
```

We have to include the **write** explicitly because this query will not succeed. It is doomed to ultimate failure because of the last subgoal **fail**, so there can be no solutions for the top-level interpreter to report. We have introduced two more built-in (or system) predicates: **nl**, which makes the output go to the start of a new line, and **fail**, which does just that, and forces the interpreter to try to find another way to satisfy the goal(s) preceding its use. The result of the query is:

```
kestrel
peregrine
no
```

As the interpreter has no entry in the database for **fail, ?- fail.** will produce **no**. The precise way the interpreter processes the query is shown below. It is extremely important that you fully comprehend the following: if you can understand it completely then you have learnt a very significant and substantial part of Prolog as this basic search strategy is used throughout Prolog:

- Satisfy the first subgoal, **falcon(X)** – it does this by searching the database and matching (instantiating) the variable X with kestrel.
- Satisfy the second subgoal, **write(kestrel)** – the X has been instantiated to kestrel and it is written to the screen.
- Satisfy the third subgoal, **nl** – the cursor goes to a new line.
- Satisfy the fourth subgoal, **fail** – there is no entry for **fail** so it fails. Resatisfy the query from the point where the last match was made – this is called "backtracking". Search the database for a match with **falcon(X)** from the entry after **falcon(kestrel)**. It succeeds by instantiating X to peregrine, using the second database entry.
- Satisfy the next subgoal, **write(X)** – **peregrine** is written.
- Satisfy the next subgoal, **nl** – the cursor goes to a new line.
- Satisfy the next subgoal, **fail** – fails.
- Resatisfy the query from the point where the last instantiation was made: fails because there are no more database entries of the form **falcon**.

This is why the final response to the query is **no**. As a total query it failed despite giving us the values we wanted. This is a perfectly legitimate way of doing things, and we will often use fail to give us this kind of result. In fact it is such a common construct that it has a name: whenever fail is used to force all the solutions to a goal it is called a *failure-driven loop*.

When a goal is satisfied against an entry in the database it "remembers" which entry satisfied it so that it can go on to look for another match should backtracking require it.

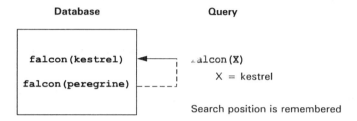

falcon(kestrel)
falcon(peregrine)

falcon(X)
X = kestrel

Search position is remembered

1.6 Prolog's search strategy

The action by which a previous instantiation is undone and the database search continued from some previously reached point is called *backtracking* and is a very important feature of Prolog. In general, Prolog's *search strategy* is to try to solve a set of subgoals from left to right, but, when one fails, it backtracks to the last possible point at which there was a choice in solving a subgoal, then, having solved it again, it continues forward through the subgoals until it fails again or until it satisfies all of the subgoals.

You should remember that **fail** is a system predicate (built-in function) whose function is to force backtracking. We could obtain the same results from our query above by replacing the use of **fail** by any subgoal that we know would fail, e.g. **?- falcon(X),write(X),nl,blue.**, where **blue** is used in place of **fail**. However, because the interpreter recognizes **fail** as a system predicate, it backtracks immediately, whereas, if any other subgoal is used, the interpreter will search the database looking for a match with that subgoal, and only when it fails to find a match will it backtrack. Because it is a system predicate, an attempt to enter **fail** as a fact in the database will not succeed.

Finally, to leave the interpreter there is a predicate **halt**. Type:

    ?- halt.

and you will be returned to the operating system. On the Windows version you can get the same result by selecting "Exit" from the "File" menu. On the Archimedes you may exit Prolog by choosing "Quit" from the menu of the bar icon.

11

Exercises 1a

1. Why is Prolog suitable for knowledge representation?
2. Complete the following:
   (a) Rules in English are characterized by the presence of the word
   _____.
   (b) Facts are stored in Prolog's internal _____.
   (c) When a variable is matched to a constant, the variable becomes
   _____ to the constant.
   (d) _____ is when the interpreter attempts to solve a query in a
   different way because a subgoal has failed.
   (e) The process by which rules are selected by matching variables and
   constants is called _____.
   (f) Constants in Prolog are often called _____.
   (g) Functions such as **fail** and **write** are usually referred to as
   _____.
3. What might be the Prolog representation for the fact that an elm is a
   kind of tree.
4. Enter three facts that represent three different types of tree into
   Prolog's database and use **write** , **nl** and **fail** in a query to output all
   three tree types on different lines.

1.7 More complex facts

A fact may have any number of arguments that may be thought of as fields
in a database record. Depending on the use we wish to put the fact to, we
give it the appropriate number of arguments. For example, if we want to
record some facts about cars, so that we might assess them for insurance
purposes, we might decide we need the following information for each
car: the manufacturer, the model, the trim (gl, xl, gt, etc.), the country of
origin, the engine capacity, the body classification (saloon, coupé, etc.) and
the purchase price (say in pounds sterling). In database terminology we
have an entity called "car" with attributes: "manufacturer", "model",
"trim", etc.

Use an editor to create a file containing the following facts:

```
car(ford,fiesta,popular,uk,950,hatchback,5300).
car(ford,orion,gl,uk,1300,saloon,7800).
car(ford,orion,gl,uk,1600,saloon,8600).
car(ford,orion,ghia,uk,1600,saloon,9500).
car(fiat,uno,55,italy,950,hatchback,5200).
car(fiat,uno,70,italy,1050,hatchback,6500).
car(rover,metro,city,uk,1000,hatchback,4900).
car(rover,metro,mg,uk,1300,hatchback,5700).
```

Use whatever editor suits you. PC users often use file extensions (such as **.pl**) to record that particular files are Prolog programs. When completed the file can be consulted using the **consult** predicate.

If you have set up a **prolog.ini** file containing the code for **edit** as detailed in section 4.5, you can, from within Keylink Prolog, type **?- edit('cars.pl').**, where **cars.pl** is the name of the file to contain the facts. When you quit the editor, the file will be read into Prolog (thus obviating the need to consult the file) and you will be back at the **?-** prompt. Archimedes users can use the CLI command:

```
settype yourfile kprolog
```

to change a file to have the Prolog program icon (where **yourfile** is the name of the file to be changed). Archimedes files may be changed back to type text by:

```
settype yourfile text
```

Using an editor will enable you to keep a Prolog database in a normal file between Prolog sessions, avoiding the need to retype large chunks of data.

From within Prolog you can read these facts into the internal database using **?- consult(filename).** If the file name has any non-alphanumeric characters, you must remember to surround it in single quotes, e.g. **?- consult('filename.pl').** If you want to refer to the file using upper-case letters you will also need to enclose it in single quotes. In the Windows and Archimedes versions you can also drag and drop the file into the Prolog window. We can then query this database in order to answer the following questions.

(a) Which cars cost less than £6000?

Prolog has the usual arithmetic comparison operators (but note the last of these, as <= is usual in other languages!): X < Y succeeds if X is arithmetically less than Y; X > Y succeeds if X is greater than Y; X >= Y succeeds if X is greater than or equal to Y; and X =< Y succeeds if X is less than or equal to Y.

```
?- car(Man,Mod,Trim,Origin,Cc,Type,Price),
   (Price < 6000).
```

This gives the result:

```
Man = ford
Mod = fiesta
Trim = popular
Origin = uk
Cc = 950
Type = hatchback
Price = 5300
```

A quick summary of how this is obtained is as follows. The first subgoal is satisfied by the first fact, which causes **Price** to have the value (be instantiated to) 5300. The second subgoal then succeeds because 5300 is less than 6000, at which point Prolog writes the values. More solutions can then be obtained by using **;**, or responding to the **Another solution** dialogue.

(b) Which saloon cars are made in the UK?

```
?- car(Man,Mod,Trim,uk,Cc,saloon,Price).
```

Notice how constants and variables are mixed in this query. We can replace those variables in which we are not interested by the underscore character, _, which is often known as the anonymous variable, as in this next query:

(c) Who manufactures the Uno?

This would be represent in Prolog as follows:

```
?- car(Man,uno,_,_,_,_,_).
```

We can make two queries together as in (d).

(d) Which two manufacturers make cars of 1300 cc capacity?

```
?- car(Man1,_,_,_,1300,_,_),
       car(Man2,_,_,_,1300,_,_),
       not(Man1 = Man2).
```

Here we have used the internal predicates **not(X)** and **=** to ensure that we do not get the same manufacturer in both cases. The predicate **not(X)** will fail if the goal X succeeds, otherwise **not(X)** succeeds. The **=** operator tests whether the terms on either side of it *match,* and is *not* used for assigning values to variables as it is in other languages. Two terms match (unify) if:
   (a) they are identical, or
   (b) the variables in each term may be instantiated in such a way that after the instantiations the terms are then identical.
Thus, **not(Man1 = Man2)** will fail if **Man1** and **Man2** match, ensuring that we get two different manufacturers. Remember that a variable can be matched with any constant and when it is matched to a constant it becomes instantiated to the constant. The variable can only subsequently become uninstatiated (a true variable again) by backtracking to a point that is previous to the original match.

   Note that the more technical term for match is *unify,* and we say that X = Y succeeds when X and Y are *unifiable.* We call the process of matching *unification.*

Exercises 1b

1. Give the result of queries (b) and (c) made in the preceding section.
2. Give a detailed account of how the result to the fourth query, (d), in the preceding section is reached, and state where backtracking occurs.
3. Using the above database on cars, make the following queries:
   (a) Find details of all cars manufactured by Ford.
   (b) Find a Ford saloon car of greater than 1300 cc capacity costing less than £9000.
   (c) Find all the Rover cars that cost more than any Fiat car.
4. We may have a relation with two arguments such as **pop(uk,55)**. which we may take to mean "The population of the UK is 55 (million)". We must use lower case for the start of the country names or the interpreter would mistake them for variables. Input a small database of five or six entries giving the population of countries in this form (approximate populations for some countries in millions are China 830, India 600, USA 210). Query the database to give you a list of the countries and their populations.
5. Write a query that will return all those countries with a population greater than 100 million.

1.8 Relating facts

We may define a new set of facts that can tell us the address and telephone number of the supplier for each manufacturer for each country as in:

```
supplier(ford,uk,'21 Tinsgate, Dagenham','0181 233 4821').
supplier(rover,uk,'18 Beadle Road, Cowley','01325 24112').
supplier(fiat,italy,'333 Via Alphonse, Turin','0101 888 376⌐
   3983').
```

We have enclosed the address and telephone fields in single quotes to enable us to include characters that would not normally be legal for a constant, such as spaces. In the same way we can also start a string with an upper-case letter if we wish. Be careful only to use singly quoted strings at this stage, as the double quotation mark has a very different purpose.

The new set of facts, **supplier**, can be used in conjunction with the old set, **cars**. For example we might make a query: What is the address of the supplier of the metro?

```
?- car(Man,metro,_,_,_,_,_),
      supplier(Man,_,Address,_).
```

Notice that the variable **Man** in the first field of the **car** subgoal is the same variable as is used in the first field in the **supplier** subgoal. This query is solved by searching the **car** set of facts until a match with **metro** in the second field is found. At this point **Man** becomes instantiated to **rover**. Then the second subgoal to the query is tried until a match is found in the supplier set of facts, with **Man** thus instantiated. This causes **Address** to become instantiated with the second fact of the supplier set. Finally, the value of **Address** is written by the top-level interpreter.

Consider the query:

```
?- car(Man,Model,_,_,_,_,_),
       supplier(Man,_,Address,_).
```

This query is capable of finding the address of the manufacturer of each car by backtracking after each solution is found. The query will start with the **car** goal matching on the first **car** fact, which will instantiate **Man** to **ford**. The second goal will then be **supplier(ford,_,Address,_)**, which will match on the supplier entry for **ford**, at which point our variable values are displayed.

We can now force backtracking in the usual way, i.e. by typing **;** as each solution is found (or responding to a dialogue). This will cause the goal **supplier(ford,_,Address,_)** to be retried. There are no more matching supplier entries for **ford**, so it will fail, thus causing backtracking to the **car(Man,Model,_,_,_,_,_)** goal, which will be satisfied on the second car fact in the database, and so the process continues through all the cars.

In many ways this is like having a loop within a loop in a conventional language, where the outer loop is over all the cars and the inner loop is for each supplier.

To take the analogy further, there would need to be an **if** statement inside the innermost loop to test that the manufacturer, represented by the variable **Man**, matched for the two sets of facts. Conventionally we might express this as:

```
for all cars do
    for all suppliers do
        if car.manufacturer=supplier.manufacturer then
            output car.model, manufacturer.address
        endif
    next supplier
next car
```

You must be very careful to understand how the backtracking is working in this example as it is entirely central to Prolog's execution model. Be alert to the fact that the occurrence of a simple goal such as **car(Man,Model,_,_,_,_,_)**, as in the previous example, implies a search on *all* car entries in the database and may be satisfied once, many times or not at all depending on the contents of the database *and* the instantiations of the variables.

If you are familiar with databases you will recognize this operation as equivalent to a database join (or more accurately an equijoin). As with databases, the significant point is that a value is used from one relation (table or set of facts) to make a match on another relation (table or set of facts), thus linking two sets of facts together.

Exercises 1c

1. Write the solutions for the above two queries.
2. Write the queries for:
   (a) Find the address of the supplier of the Metro MG.
   (b) Find all the names and telephone numbers of saloon car suppliers in the UK.
   (c) Find the telephone numbers of all the suppliers of cars with engine capacity greater than 1300 cc.

CHAPTER TWO
Rules

2.1 Introduction to rules

The power of programming in Prolog is achieved by the use of rules. In a general sense, i.e. not just when talking about Prolog, a rule in its simplest form consists of:

    A if B

where A and B stand for goals. That is, to achieve goal A, achieve goal B. We often think in terms of proving a goal, so we might read this as: to prove goal A (to be true) we must prove goal B (to be true). This is just another way of saying that goal A is implied by goal B. Yet another way to describe the same thing is "If B then A". It is important to realize that these are equivalent ways of expressing the same relationship between B and A.

It is more usual for a rule to take the form:

    A if B and C

or:

    A if B and C and D and ...

That is, to achieve goal A, achieve goal B and then achieve goal C and so on, for all the goals on the right-hand side of the **if**. Or, to prove goal A we must prove goal B, goal C and so on.

The idea of proving does not necessarily involve any order in which we look at B and C: this is called the *declarative semantics*. However, when we talk about achieving goals, we need to know the order in which to attempt them: this is the *procedural semantics* and corresponds to the order that the interpreter will attempt to solve the goals. We often call the goals occurring on the right-hand side of the **if** subgoals. The goal on the left-hand side of the **if** is called the *head* of the rule, while the subgoals following the **if** are known collectively as the *body* of the rule.

This kind of construct, with more than one subgoal, enables us to break large goals into smaller subgoals with much the same kind of benefit that we get from modularity in conventional languages. In fact, if you are familiar with top-down design of conventional software engineering, then you already have an effective tool with which to design large Prolog rule bases.

We express rules in Prolog by using the symbol `:-` for **if**, and the `,` (comma) to represent **and**. A very simple rule in Prolog is:

```
i_play_tennis:-
    it_is_saturday,
    weather_is_fine.
```

Note the layout used in writing this rule: the head appears on one line, with each subgoal appearing on a separate line and indented from the rule head. As in more conventional languages, using this kind of layout aids program legibility and debugging.

This is a very simple rule because it uses no variables. It consists of a proposition **i_play_tennis** which can be proved by establishing (finding in the database) the two simple propositions **it_is_saturday** and **weather_is_fine**. Therefore the query:

```
?- i_play_tennis.
```

will have the response **yes** only if:

```
    it_is_saturday.
    weather_is_fine.
```

are present in the database. This is not quite true, as we could replace these facts by more rules. For example instead of **weather_is_fine** occurring as a fact, we could have the rule:

```
weather_is_fine:-
    sunny,
    not(raining).
```

Now for the query `?- i_play_tennis.` to be satisfied the database would need the fact **sunny**, but *not* the fact **raining**. Something not being true is represented in Prolog by its absence, or by reason of there being no proof of it. (This is sometimes called the "closed world assumption" .) If **something** is not in the database and it cannot be derived from the contents of the database then **not(something)** will succeed.

The solution tree for this looks like:

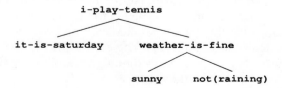

Each leaf node (the ones at the extremes) would need to match against a fact in the database, except for the one preceded by not, which must not exist in the database. The tree is constructed quite simply, by starting with the goal and writing the subgoals that must be satisfied underneath and left to right. This is repeated for all the subgoals. This is effectively hand tracing what the Prolog system does, and is an extremely effective way to gain an understanding of the execution behaviour of a Prolog query.

The problem with simple propositions such as **weather_is_fine** is that they are too restrictive. We cannot usefully express any rule that concerns a class of objects, such as "All men are mortal". Although we can express this as a proposition, e.g. in Prolog:

```
all_men_are_mortal.
```

this does not enable us to derive, given a particular man, that he is mortal. That is, if we add:

```
napoleon_is_a_man.
```

it is impossible for Prolog to derive that Napoleon is mortal. This is because propositions have to be dealt with as a whole. However, Prolog allows us to overcome this difficulty by the use of variables: the simple rule in Prolog that involves variables and corresponds to this rule is:

```
mortal(X):-
    man(X).
```

which we can translate back into "To prove that X is mortal you must prove that X is a man" or "If X is a man then X must be mortal". (Take great care over the direction of the implication intended: in Prolog the conclusion is on the left, that is it is the head of the rule.) This amounts to "All men are mortal" because, as far as Prolog is concerned, this means all men that Prolog knows about (this is the closed world assumption!). If we add the facts:

```
man(john).
man(peter).
```

and enter the query:

```
?- mortal(X).
```

and ask for all the solutions by using the semicolon or responding to the dialogue, we get the answers:

```
john
peter
```

This works by **mortal(X)** being matched with the head (left-hand side of **:-**) and then an attempt is made to satisfy the subgoals in the body of the rule (those goals to the right of **:-**). In this case there is only one, namely **man(X)**. **man(X)** is satisfied by matching with **man(john)** in the database, and thus **mortal(X)** is satisfied. Then the value that X is instantiated to, i.e. **john**, is written. The semicolon causes backtracking to the last

21

point where there was an alternative solution, so **man(X)** is resatisfied with
man(peter), **mortal(X)** is solved again, the instantiation is written and finally the query fails as there are no more alternatives (these are also called
backtrack or choice points).

The solution tree for the first solution is:

```
?- mortal(X).
     |
  mortal(X)
     |
  man(X)
     |  {X = john}
  man(john)
```

Note that this shows the query goal being matched against the head of
the rule and then the subgoal in the body of the rule being matched against
a fact.

We can add facts that use **mortal** directly, such as:

```
mortal(gordon).
mortal(mary).
```

and our query **?- mortal(X).** will now give us the response:

```
john
peter
gordon
mary
```

Can you explain the order of the output?

To summarize, a rule consists of a head and a body joined by Prolog's
if, which is represented by **:-**. Where there is more than one subgoal to be
solved in the body of the rule, these are separated by a comma, which represents **and**. The head of a rule can match a subgoal being solved at run
time in the same way that a fact can. But, for this subgoal to succeed, the
body of the rule must be satisfied, that is each subgoal to the right of the **:-**
must be taken in turn and solved, again, either by matching on the heads
of rules, in which case their bodies must be solved, or by matching on
facts.

A very simple but useful rule is to define **writeln** as:

```
writeln(X) :-
    write(X),
    nl.
```

nl was introduced in the previous chapter, and forces subsequent output to begin on a new line: thus **writeln(X)** will write the value of X and
then go to a new line. This is so useful I will often assume that it has been
defined and you might like to consider putting it in your **prolog.ini** file.

It is more normal for rules to have more than one subgoal on the right-hand side, as in the following two examples:

```
buys(X,Y) :-
    can_afford(X, Y),
    has_need_of(X, Y).
bird(X) :-
    vertebrate(X),
    feathered(X).
```

The first example can be read as "X will buy Y if X can afford Y and X has need of Y" and the second, completely in English, as "A bird is a feathered vertebrate".

2.2 Execution tracing

If you have entered a query and it does not give the result you expect, you can follow the execution of the query with the trace predicate. There are slight differences between the use of trace on the PC DOS , Windows and Archimedes versions. If you are using Windows or an Archimedes read this section through to the end before trying an example.

When you enter:

```
?- trace.
```

every query entered will now have its execution trace printed on the screen. This shows which rules and facts are being used to solve the query and which variable instantiations have been made at any particular point. It does not affect your normal output. After each line of output from the debugger reply with <Enter> to allow the trace to continue. It is strongly recommended that while you are at the initial stages of learning Prolog you use the trace predicate often. If you want to stop tracing the execution of your queries type:

```
?- notrace.
```

The following is an example of trace being used with the following database:

```
bird(X):-
    vertebrate(X),
    feathered(X).
vertebrate(cat).
vertebrate(kestrel).
feathered(pillow).
feathered(kestrel).
?- trace.
yes
?- bird(X).
```

```
1 Call: bird(_28101)
2    Call: vertebrate(_28102)
2    Exit: vertebrate(cat)
2    Call: feathered(cat)
2    Fail: feathered(cat)
2    Redo: vertebrate(_28102)
2    Call: vertebrate(_28102)
2    Exit: vertebrate(kestrel)
2    Call: feathered(kestrel)
2    Exit: feathered(kestrel)
1 Exit: bird(kestrel)
X = kestrel
yes
?- notrace.
1 Call: notrace
yes
```

The **trace** is indented so that we can identify the calls with the corresponding exits. Each invocation of a goal or subgoal is labelled **Call**. The successful solution of a called goal is labelled **Exit**, failure is labelled **Fail** and, where this causes backtracking to occur, it is indicated by **Redo**. Note that variables are not printed in their original form. When a rule is being used by the Prolog system it has memory allocated to each of its variables that relate to this and only this use of the rule. The numbers printed out in place of the variable names are pointers to these allocations. Although this may seem obscure, it does not, in practice, make any difference. We can still identify which variable is meant and its subsequent occurrences.

The search strategy of Prolog described in the previous chapter is reflected in the above trace. Prolog starts with the goal of the query, **bird(X)**, and matches it against the head of a rule or a fact. Prolog proceeds from left to right through the subgoals, attempting to solve each in turn. A failure causes backtracking to the most recent choice point. In the example, **feathered(cat)** fails and backtracking allows **vertebrate(X)** to be retried, whereupon it is matched with **vertebrate(kestrel)** and execution continues forward. This description of Prolog execution strategy is known as the procedural semantics of Prolog. It describes what Prolog actually does at execution time. In particular, the ordering of subgoals is of paramount importance. This is in contrast to what are known as the declarative semantics, in which we are only interested in the relationships established by the rules without reference to the sequence in which they will be executed.

As well as pressing <Enter> at each line of the trace, there are a further three meaningful responses: <s> for **skip** , <n> for **notrace** and <r> for **run** all the execution with trace output (i.e. do not stop for debugger responses). **skip** tells Prolog to solve the current goal without showing any trace output and to return to trace when it is either solved or fails. **notrace** switches tracing off.

Windows Prolog gives you the same options via a dialogue:

Here **All** is equivalent to <r> and we have the extra option of quitting (aborting) the query.

On the Archimedes a dialogue box appears with three buttons for **step**, **Skip** and **stop** tracing.

Clicking **step** will cause the query to be solved while displaying trace information at each stage of its solution; **skip** tells Prolog to solve the current subgoal without displaying trace information, then return to trace mode, and **stop Tracing** switches tracing off, and the initial goal is solved with no more trace information being displayed. Tracing on the Archimedes is covered in more detail in the Appendix C.

As an additional aid to code development, Prolog will issue a warning whenever a *singleton variable* is detected in a clause. A singleton variable is one that occurs only once in a clause. For example, if the rule for **bird** above was written thus:

```
bird(Y):-
    vertebrate(X),
    feathered(X).
```

then a warning will be issued for **Y: singleton var# 1 in bird/1**, where **var# 1** means the first variable in the clause. By default, warnings are switched off. In order to be able to see warnings you must use:

```
?- warnings(on).
```

2.3 Rules for the car database

Let us return to the car database used in the previous chapter. If we were developing a system to assign a given car to its correct insurance group automatically, what sort of rules would we expect? It is common for a points system to be used. The points that a particular car gains are a result of a variety of its attributes, and it is the number of points that determines its risk category or insurance group. For our first rule we will take the engine capacity as the relevant attribute: the higher the capacity, the more points the car will score. For example:

```
risk_for_capacity(Capacity, 1):-
    Capacity < 1000.
risk_for_capacity(Capacity, 2):-
    Capacity >= 1000,
    Capacity < 1300.
risk_for_capacity(Capacity, 3):-
    Capacity >= 1300,
    Capacity < 1500.
risk_for_capacity(Capacity, 4):-
    Capacity >= 1500,
    Capacity < 2000.
risk_for_capacity(Capacity, 5):-
    Capacity >= 2000,
    Capacity < 3500.
risk_for_capacity(Capacity, 6):-
    Capacity >= 3500.
```

The points value is the second argument. Note that it does not need to be assigned in any way in the body of the rule, which would be extremely poor Prolog style.

A single one of these rules is called a *clause*. A set of clauses all with the same head is known collectively as a single rule. Thus we have a single **risk_for_capacity** rule comprising six clauses. It is quite usual for a large set of clauses to exist for a rule, all having the same head, as in this example.

All clauses for a rule should be contiguous to aid readability. If the clauses for a rule are separated by clauses for a different rule you will get a warning from the Prolog system.

The **risk_for_capacity** rule allows us to make the following type of query: How many points are assigned to a capacity of 1800 cc?

```
?- risk_for_capacity(1800, Points).
```

This has the solution tree:

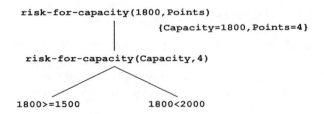

This shows the successful match with the fourth clause, which is achieved by backtracking each time one of the conditions fails in the first three clauses. Notice that the search strategy that has been given applies to backtracking over the clauses in the rules. In the above example `risk_for_capacity(1800, Points)` is matched against the first clause, but then allows the next clause to be tried.

The solution tree gives us a diagrammatic representation of how a solution can be derived from the known rules and facts. The solution tree is a diagrammatic representation of the proof of the goal and, as such, is an extremely powerful mental model. You should try to draw solution trees whenever your understanding of a goal sequence is less than perfect. Being able to draw reliable proof trees enables you to hand execute Prolog, and this is a powerful test of your understanding. This is also a very useful exercise when you cannot test your code against a Prolog system, such as in an exam! Some guidelines on drawing solution trees will be given as we meet more complicated examples.

We can find the points for `risk_for_capacity` for all cars by making the query:

```
?- car(Man, Model, Trim, _, Cc, _, _),
    risk_for_capacity(Cc, Points).
```

We can define a rule that uses both the car and supplier facts. For example, we might need a rule that found the price and the supplier's address for a given car, where we supplied the manufacturer, the model, the trim and the capacity.

```
price_and_address(Man, Mod, Trim, Cap, Price, Address):-
    car(Man, Mod, Trim, Origin, Cap, _, Price),
    suppliers(Man, Origin, Address, _).
```

2.4 Arithmetic

Perhaps surprisingly, you can get a long way into Prolog before doing any arithmetic, which is generally the first thing you learn in any other computer language. To add or compute any arithmetic expression in Prolog you need to use the **is** predicate, which is used for arithmetic assignment. For example, the query:

```
?- X is (12 + 9).
```

instantiates X to 21, in the same way that the assignment operators = or := may be used in other languages, with one very important difference, which will be discussed in the next chapter.

The normal arithmetic operators are supported: * for multiply, / for divide, + for add and - for minus. In addition, there are two "bit-shift operators": <<, which performs a left-shift, and >>, which shifts right.

These shift left or right the bit-pattern that represents the number to the left of the operator by the number of bits specified on the right of the operator, thus:

```
?- X is (1 << 1). /* 0001 << 1 = 0010 = 2 */
X = 2
?- X is (12 >> 2). /* 1100 >> 2 = 0011 = 3 */
X = 3
```

Note the two comments in the above code. Comments are introduced with /* and terminated with */. Such comments may extend over one or more lines, all text between the opening /* and the closing */ being ignored by the interpreter. Alternatively, a comment may be started with %, but will then only extend to the end of the line; thus there is no need for a termination character. The liberal use of comments is strongly recommended as an aid to program comprehension.

We can define a rule that determines the discounted price of a car using **is** to do a simple bit of arithmetic. Say we are offering a 10% discount for cash:

```
discount_for_cash(Fullprice,Cutprice):-
    Cutprice is Fullprice * 0.9.
```

We will meet **is** again in the next chapter, where it will be discussed more thoroughly.

Exercises 2

1. The left-hand part of a rule is called the rule _____ while the subgoals on the right-hand side are called the _____ of the rule.
2. Draw the solution tree for the **bird(X)** query whose execution is shown traced in section 2.2.
3. Experiment with the buys and bird rules, introducing your own facts and queries until you feel perfectly at home with them and can effortlessly predict the results of your queries.
4. Put the following facts into Prolog's database:

```
event(battle_of_hastings, 1066).
event(plague_of_london, 1665).
event(fire_of_london, 1666).
event(man_on_the_moon, 1969).
```

Define a rule **happened_before(X,Y)** that defines the relation that event X happened before event Y and use it to obtain all such pairs of events. You will need to use the system predicate <, less than. For example ?- (5 < 7). succeeds. Suitably instantiated variables can be used either side of < instead of numbers. Start the rule with **happened_before(X,Y) :-** .

5. Tom dislikes anyone in the third year who likes Dave. Dave only likes hard workers and first years. Pete and Nigel are in the first year, Sam and Jane are in the third year. Sam and Pete dislike Dave and like Tom. Jane likes Dave. Pete, Nigel and Jane are all hard workers. Use Prolog to express the facts and rules (remember to start the students' names with a lower-case letter) and find out: Who does Tom dislike?

6. Introduce the following car facts into the database alongside those we have met previously:

```
car(ford, capri, injection,uk, 2800, sports, 11200).
car(alfa_romeo, sprint, veloce, italy, 2000, coupe,⏎
    12500).
car(volvo, 928, gls, sweden, 1400, hatchback, 6290).
car(mitsubishi, colt, glx, japan, 1800, estate,⏎
    7420).
car(mercedes, roadster, 280, germany, 2800, convert-⏎
    ible, 18450).
```

Write a set of facts that gives points for the type of car body according to the following table:

Type	Points
estate	1
saloon	2
hatchback	1
sports	3
coupé	5
convertible	7

7. Write a rule that uses the facts and the `risk_for_capacity` rule already described to determine the total points scored by a car for engine capacity and body type. This will entail adding together the points for the capacity and the points for the body type. The car is to be identified by the manufacturer and model.

CHAPTER THREE

Recursive rules

3.1 Simple example of recursion

Recursive rules are simply rules that call themselves. Defining a rule in terms of itself can lead to very elegant and concise programs. Many mathematical functions can be expressed recursively, the most common example being the factorial function denoted by an exclamation mark. But before doing the factorial example, we will look at one of the simplest examples possible that involves recursion. The problem is to move the cursor a given number of spaces towards the right of the screen, and we might use this rule to format our output. Such a function is commonly called **tab**, short for tabulate. However, there is already a built-in predicate called **tab** so we will call our rule **spaces**. An example of its use is:

```
write_headings:-
    spaces(20),
    writeln('MANUFACTURER MODEL PRICE').
```

(Notice that I am assuming **writeln** has been defined.) This rule would move the cursor 20 spaces to the right before printing the text and going to a new line.

Remember from the previous chapter how to assign a numeric value to a variable: this is effected by the **is** predicate, which we will now explain a little more fully. The **is** built-in predicate is an "infix" operator, that is it comes between its arguments, e.g.

```
?- X is 29, writeln(X).
?- X is 777 * 5, writeln(X).
```

The fact that it is defined as being infix is a matter of convenience. It might have been defined as "prefix", i.e. coming before its arguments. All the predicates we have used so far have been prefix, the "car" predicate for example. If **is** were to be prefix, the first of the above queries would

31

need to be written as:

```
?- is(X,29),writeln(X).
```

It is obviously more convenient to use the infix form. Notice that an infix operator or predicate must have precisely two arguments.

As stated in the previous chapter, **is** is rather like = in other languages. However, the left-hand side of **is** must be an uninstantiated variable, i.e. it must not already have a value, or it must be equal to the value of the expression to its right. This is known as *non-destructive* assignment, which is really a consequence of logic that insists that we cannot arbitrarily reassign values to variables that might change the truth value of a statement. Thus, the following query:

```
?- X is 4, write(X), X is X + 1, write(X).
```

will fail at the **X is X + 1** subgoal because 4 is not 5. Soon we will see how to get round this when we need to increment a numeric value.

Remember that, although = is defined in Prolog, it does not have the meaning of assignment, so if you use it where **is** is required you will not get the desired result! A query such as:

```
?- X = 1 + 2.
```

will result in Prolog replying:

```
X = 1 + 2
```

as = is used as a "matching" operator, as detailed in Chapter 2, and here causes X to be matched to 1 + 2 which is a *structure*, something we will see a lot more of in later chapters.

All recursive programs, whether written in Prolog or some other language, have two basic parts. The first consists of what to do when there is to be no more recursion, which we call the *boundary case*. In this example, the boundary case is when there are no more spaces to be printed. The other part consists of what to do in the *general case*, followed by some alteration to the parameters and then a call to the same rule or subprogram. In a conventional language we would distinguish the two cases within the same program by using an "if . . . then . . . else . . ." type of statement, but in Prolog we use unification (the matching of the arguments) to select the correct clause.

We start the rule by considering the boundary case for spaces, i.e. the case where there is nothing to do, that is when **spaces(0)** is the subgoal. Here we simply want the query to be satisfied and nothing more to happen. Therefore the first clause of our rule is:

```
spaces(0).
```

This will clearly match with **spaces(N)** whenever N is instantiated to 0, and will cause nothing to happen because there is nothing in the clause's body to execute (a fact is nothing other than a clause without a body).

In the general case, we need to write a space and then reinvoke spaces with an argument that corresponds to a count of one space fewer, e.g.:

```
spaces(N):-
    N > 0,
    write(' '),
    M is N - 1,
    spaces(M).
```

The first subgoal makes sure the number represented by N is valid: this is good programming practice and may prevent unwelcome results. Consider what would otherwise happen if N were inadvertently instantiated to a negative number.

To illustrate how this rule works, consider the query:

```
?- spaces(2).
```

1. This matches the second clause, so a single space is printed, then
2. M is calculated to be 1 and **spaces(1)** is called.
3. **spaces(1)** matches the second clause and so another space is printed, then
4. M is calculated to be 0 and **spaces(0)** is called.
5. **spaces(0)** is satisfied by the first clause and the query has been satisfied completely.

Note how a different variable to N is used for the calculation of the argument to the next call of spaces, to circumvent Prolog's non-destructive assignment: attempting to use **N is N-1** would fail. As a general rule, whenever you want a new value based on that of another variable, such as incrementing and decrementing numbers, then use a new variable for this value.

The solution tree for the query is:

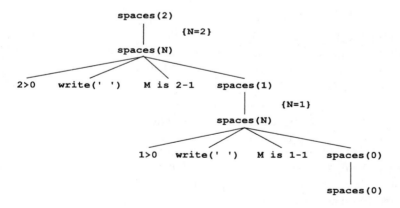

I have indicated the unifications in curly brackets; the variables in the subgoals beneath the unification are then shown to reflect the result of this unification. Writing out the unifications explicitly helps us in eliminating errors. It makes the process of drawing such a tree more mechanical and hence less error prone.

Recursion causes severe difficulties for some people as they fail to understand how a function can be executing more than once at any one time. Well this is really looking at the problem the wrong way. Each call to a recursive procedure is using a copy of the original procedure that to all intents and purposes could just as well be called something different. i.e. the recursive calls could be to **spaces1** and then **spaces2** and so on. If they were called **spaces1, spaces2**, there would not be, of course, any recursion, and therefore nothing to get confused about! It is vital to realize that the recursive calls are using copies of the original, each of which has its own set of variables and its own position in the execution path to return to. There is nothing inherently complex about recursion, it is just that we get overfamiliar with how non-recursive calls work, which gives us an incomplete mental model that is hard to extend to the recursive cases.

3.2 Calculating factorials

Now for the more complicated factorial example.

For those who have not heard of the factorial function, the factorial of a number is the number obtained when you take the number and multiply it by one less than the number, and then by two less, etc. until you reach zero, and is denoted by the exclamation mark. Thus, $5! = 5 * 4 * 3 * 2 * 1 = 120$. By convention, $0!$ is taken to be 1.

The recursive definition of factorial function is:

$$N! = N * (N - 1)!$$
$$0! = 1$$

which we can read as "The factorial of a number N is N times the factorial of N–1, and the factorial of 0 is 1". It should be fairly clear that this information is just exactly enough to calculate any factorial number. For instance, to calculate 4! using this definition and absolutely no insight, we might calculate as follows:

$4! = 4 * 3!$	using the first statement
$4! = 4 * 3 * 2!$	using the first statement
$4! = 4 * 3 * 2 * 1!$	using the first statement
$4! = 4 * 3 * 2 * 1 * 0!$	using the first statement
$4! = 4 * 3 * 2 * 1 * 1$	using the second statment
$4! = 24$	using multiplication

(The definition assumed that we knew how to multiply.)

In Prolog we cannot define a function whose name returns a value, as we can in other languages, such as in:

```
X = fact(Y).
```

so we use another argument for the value to be returned, which makes it look more like a subroutine or procedure than a function.

We first define the factorial of 0 as 1:

```
fact(0, 1).
```

This is the boundary case. Always start defining a recursive rule by considering the boundary case; it makes defining the recursive part very much easier as you can see what the recursion should be aiming at. Each step of the recursion, i.e. each recursive call, should take you one step nearer to satisfying the boundary clause.

Then we use the first part of the definition to give us the rule:

```
fact(N, X) :-
    N > 0,
    X1 is N - 1,
    fact(X1, X2),
    X is N * X2.
```

Again we check that N is in the range that we wish this clause to deal with. This follows the definition very closely. It looks rather different because we have to re-express it in the syntax of Prolog. We can now ask Prolog to calculate a factorial by a query of the form:

```
?- fact(3, X).
```

Let us hand trace the execution of this query:
1. **fact(3, X)** matches with **fact(N, X)** with N = 3.
2.   Subgoal **N > 0** succeeds.
3.   Subgoal **X1 is N-1** instantiates X1 to 2.
4.   Subgoal **fact(2, X2)** is called.
5.   **fact(2, X2)** matches with **fact(N, X)** with N = 2.
6.   Subgoal **N > 0** succeeds.
7.   Subgoal **X1 is N-1** instantiates X1 to 1.
8.   Subgoal **fact(1, X2)** is called.
9.   **fact(1, X2)** matches with **fact(N, X)** with N = 1.
10.   Subgoal **N > 0** succeeds.
11.   Subgoal **X1 is N-1** instantiates X1 to 0.
12.   Subgoal **fact(0, X2)** is called.
13.   **fact(0, X2)** matches with **fact(0, 1)** with X2 = 1.
14.   Subgoal **X is N*X2** instantiates X to 2.
15.   Subgoal **X is N*X2** instantiates X to 6.

Notice how I have used indentation to show the "depth" of the solution process.

It is a useful tip always to define the boundary condition before the general case. This can prevent infinite recursion. It is possible for the interpreter to carry on using the general case when it matches on the boundary case as well, if it finds the general case first! If the boundary condition is always before the general case, you know that the interpreter has to check whether it matches with the boundary case every time "round" the recursion regardless of whether a match with the general case is possible. This is commonly known as "defensive programming". Every effort made in making our rules "safe" will be amply rewarded in the long run.

No sane programmer would calculate factorials this way, a look-up table is considerably more efficient, but it does demonstrate a very simple use of recursion. In Prolog we have to use recursion to achieve what we would often use a loop to do in other languages, there being no iterative construct such as Basic's **FOR...NEXT**.

Exercises 3

1. Draw a solution tree for the query ?- **fact(3, X).**, using the hand trace given in the text as a guide.

2. Construct a database containing facts about the relations father and mother such as:

   ```
   father(harold, charles).
   mother(harold, diana).
   father(charles, philip).
   mother(charles, elizabeth).
   ```

   but covering a few more generations. Make up the names if necessary. Then define the recursive relation **ancestor(A, B)** that can generate the ancestors of A. [An ancestor is (i) a father, (ii) a mother, (iii) an ancestor of (i), (iv) an ancestor of (ii).]

3. Define a predicate **mod5(X, Y)** that instantiates Y to X mod 5 by recursively subtracting 5 from X. (X mod 5 gives the remainder when 5 is divided into X as many complete times as possible, for example 23 mod 5 = 3.) Start this by defining the boundary case first (this is where X <= 5).

4. Define a predicate **power(X, N, P)** that instantiates P to X raised to the power N (where N is an integer). Remember X to the power 0 is 1. Start by defining the boundary case.

5. Define a predicate that converts a number of minutes into the corresponding hours and minutes by recursively subtracting 60 from the number of minutes and incrementing the number of hours. An example of using the rule is:

   ```
   ?- mins_to_hours_and_mins(124, H, M).
   H = 2
   M = 4
   ```

CHAPTER FOUR

Survival predicates

This chapter introduces some basic built-in predicates that will help you generally as your use of Prolog becomes more advanced and you start to experiment with your own code. The type checking predicates are particularly important in writing defensive code and should be used liberally to aid your debugging. I also introduce **assert** and **retract** in this chapter. These are predicates that can be used to alter the contents of Prolog's database while the program is running. These are discussed as you are almost certain to find them being used in example programs from other sources that you may want to try.

4.1 Accessing the operating system on the PC

On the PC under DOS you can temporarily return to the operating system by using the predicate shell. This does not apply to Windows, in which you will find double clicking on the DOS icon from the Program manager a far more convenient way of running DOS.

For example to exit to the operating system when running Prolog from DOS, type **?- shell.** To return to Prolog, type **exit**. The system will respond with:

C:\PROLOG>

You may then pass commands to the operating system and run other programs in the normal way. After each command is run you will be reminded that you have suspended Prolog, and of how to resume, by the prompt **To return to Prolog type exit**. Typing **exit** followed by <Enter> will return you to the interpreter at the same point at which execution was suspended. During the period between executing the shell goal and returning to Prolog the interpreter will remain in memory, thus the memory available in which to run other programs will be reduced by that consumed by Prolog.

You can examine the contents of your directory, or execute any other single operating system command from within the interpreter, by using the system command. For example:

```
?- system('dir /w').
```

will display the contents of the current directory down and across the screen. Programs initiated through the **system** command will have available memory reduced in the same way as for **shell**. As for **shell**, **system** is not available from Windows Prolog.

Additional functionality can be gained by using **system** with strings, constructed using Prolog, that write to temporary files, then processing these files using Prolog, as demonstrated by **edit** later in this chapter.

4.2 Accessing the operating system on the Archimedes

The **system** predicate allows CLI commands to be executed from within Prolog. Note that no text output will appear in the Kprolog window, so only those CLI commands that manipulate files, directories or environment variables are appropriate. The **system** predicate is dealt with in more detail in Appendix C.

4.3 Retracting, clearing and abolishing

A fact may be retracted (removed) from the database by using the predicate **retract(X)**. It has one argument that must be instantiated to the fact that you would like to remove, e.g.

```
?- retract(falcon(kestrel)).

yes
```

Listing the database will show that the fact has been removed. Note that the fact has been removed for good: backtracking will not undo the retraction, although it can be replaced by either using **assert(X)** (see §4.4) or by typing it directly into the database using **?- consult(user)**. The argument of **retract** does not need to be fully instantiated to the fact; the *functor* (head) is sufficient. The arguments are used for unification with candidate clauses for retraction. For example:

```
?- retract(falcon(X)).
```

would retract the first match with **falcon(X)** and would also cause X to become instantiated to kestrel in the above example, if we take **falcon(kestrel)** to be the first entry in the database with the functor falcon.

A set of clauses that have the same head, or functor, may be deleted by using the **abolish(X)** predicate. For example, if the database contains:

```
falcon(kestrel).
falcon(peregrine).
crow(magpie).
```

then entering:

```
?- abolish(falcon).
```

will delete both entries for falcon and leave the one for crow. The **abolish** predicate simply searches for occurrences of the functor. We can restrict the number of clauses removed by specifying the *arity* of the clause(s). The arity of a clause is simply its number of arguments, so our falcon clauses have an arity of 1, whereas the facts for the ancestor relation in the previous chapter have an arity of 2. For example:

```
?- abolish(falcon, 1).
```

retracts all clauses having the functor **falcon** and one argument. **retract** and **abolish** are equally happy to delete rules as well as facts, so be careful!

4.4 Asserting

Facts and rules may be added (asserted) by using one of the assert predicates, **assert(X), asserta(X)** and **assertz(X)**. The difference between them is that **asserta** asserts to the start of the database, while **assert** and **assertz** assert to the end of the database, e.g.

```
?- asserta(falcon(kestrel)).
```

would make **falcon(kestrel)** the first **falcon** fact in the database.

Excessive use of **assert, asserta, assertz** and **retract** tends to make Prolog programs very difficult to read and understand. This is because they effectively modify the program, and thus tend to destroy the declarative reading of a program. Relations that are true at some points are not true at others; clauses, and indeed rules, may come and go as program execution proceeds. This causes a reading of the program, which necessarily sees it in a static state, to need to consider the procedural implications of the asserts and retracts (the dynamic effects of the alteration of the database).

A program without asserts and retracts can be very effectively read because of the declarative nature of the rules and the lack of procedural implications. So it is worth noting that we might be giving up a very useful feature of Prolog when we use **assert** and **retract**.

It is strongly suggested that the reader avoids using these predicates whenever possible. You certainly should not use **assert** and **retract** for communicating information that would normally be passed by a rule's parameters. A legitimate use is for the same kind of reason we would use a global flag in a conventional language to signal a condition of global interest. We also use **assertz** and **retract** for counting the number of occurrences of facts or particular solutions. For example, we might wish to find out how many falcons are defined in our database. This is the usual technique for counting the number of times a goal succeeds, so for our example we would call **count(falcon(X),N)**:

```
count(Goal,N):-
    assertz(count(0)),
    count1(Goal),
    retract(count(N)).
```

This initializes the counting process by asserting a count of zero, calling a subgoal to do the main part of the counting (which will be a failure-driven loop), and finally retracting the state of the last count to give the number. The rule for **count1** is:

```
count1(Goal):-
    call(Goal),
    retract(count(N)),
    M is N + 1,
    assertz(count(M)),
    fail.
count1(_).
```

call(X) is a convenient built-in predicate for calling a Prolog goal that we want to represent as a variable and instantiate at run time. In our example, **Goal** would be instantiated to **falcon(X)** and **call(Goal)** would be equivalent to **falcon(X)**. Here we have used **fail** as the last goal to force every possible solution of **Goal** to be evaluated, and for each solution we retract the current count, increment it and assert the new count. Ultimately we fail and backtrack into the second clause for **count1**, which succeeds immediately.

Another convenient application is for what is sometimes called "solution caching". This is of use when we have taken considerable effort (or rather our program has) to obtain a solution that we know we will need in the future and we do not wish to have to go through the same trouble to find it again. For instance, if I am interfacing to an external database and I need to access a particular table, then I will need to get the data dictionary information to allow the access. Rather than fetch this information each time I need it, I can cache it by asserting it to the internal database. Then, whenever I need data dictionary information, I look in the internal database first: only if it is not there do I then go and fetch it.

4.5 Editing on the PC under DOS

It is an easy matter to define a predicate that invokes an editor, which then lets you change the contents of a file and then reads the file into Prolog's database. This means that we can edit and reread our rule base without having to stop and restart Prolog.

A useful predicate for reading files, typically containing Prolog programs, into the interpreter is **reconsult(F)**, where **F** represents the name of the file in each case. Clauses read from a file through **reconsult** are always added to the database whenever clauses of the same functor and arity are not present in the database. However, if any clauses in the database have the same functor and arity as any found in the file being read, those in the database will be replaced by the new versions. Historically there is also a built-in predicate called **consult**, which is identical to **reconsult**.

This is how you may define your own version of edit:

```
edit(File):-
    name(File, Flist),
    append("vi ", Flist, L),
    name(S, L),
    system(S),
    reconsult(File).
```

This edit rule is given a single parameter that is the file name of the Prolog source code. The **name(A,L)** built-in predicate takes as its first argument an atom; the second argument is a list of the ASCII codes that make up the atom, and Prolog expects that either one, but not both, will be instantiated. Examples of its use are:

```
?- name(fred, X).
X = [102,114,101,100]
?- name(X, [102,114,101,100]).
X = fred
?- name(fred, [102,B,101,C]).
B = 114
C = 100
```

The square brackets, [ ], enclosing the ASCII codes are simply Prolog's way of writing a list: lists will be covered in detail in Chapter 7, but note here that a string enclosed in double quotes in Prolog is equivalent to the list of its ASCII codes: thus **"vi "** is another way of writing **[118,105,32]**. The rule **append(L1, L2, L3)** concatenates, or joins, lists L1 and L2 to form list L3 (see §6.3), so the **edit** rule takes the list of ASCII codes corresponding to "vi " and concatenates it with the list of ASCII codes that corresponds to the file name, to form list L. Then, using **name**, it turns this

ASCII list into an atom and calls **system** with it. This will invoke the editor with the file name you gave **edit**.

When **system** is finished, i.e. when you finish editing, the file that has just been edited is reconsulted, thus, as explained above, any existing definitions of rules in the file being reconsulted are removed from the internal database before adding the ones in the file to the database. This is exactly what we require in an editing situation where we wish to replace the old version of rules with the newly edited version.

If you intend using **edit** frequently, define a file called **prolog.ini** in your Prolog directory, or one on an **append** path, and put the definition for edit into it. This file will then be consulted every time you invoke Prolog.

4.6 Spy points

How to trace Prolog's execution using the built-in predicate **trace** was described in Chapter 2. This described the debugger in trace mode that gives complete trace information starting from the query goal. This will quite often produce far too much information for convenient analysis. More control over the tracing facility can be obtained by setting so-called spy points on particular predicates in our code. When we set a spy point on a particular predicate, the debugger will work in "debug" mode, that is execution will proceed without trace information being output until the predicate with the spy point is called. At this point the trace debugging mode is entered. If we subsequently use **run** then execution will continue without debugging information until the next spy point is reached. We can set spy points on predicates by using the built-in predicate **spy** giving the predicate name as the only argument. For example:

```
?- spy(count1).
```

We can set as many spy points as needed by calling **spy** for each spy point we want. Spy points can be removed one at a time by using **nospy**, giving the name of the predicate for its argument, or all at once using **nospyall**.

4.7 Declaring operators

The **op** predicate allows us to define new Prolog operators, which are either *infix* (coming between their arguments) or *prefix* (coming before their argument). We have already met some examples of infix and prefix operators, as well as the usual arithmetic operators that are generally infix. Note that **:-** is an infix operator coming between the head and body of a rule and **?-** is a prefix operator coming before a query.

Declaring certain Prolog functors as infix and prefix can dramatically improve the syntax of our Prolog clauses in certain situations. There are many examples of the use of **op** in Chapter 12, where it is used to implement a natural syntax for defining expert system production rules.

It is also necessary to specify an operator's *precedence* and *associativity*. The precedence determines the order of evaluation when used in a situation that would otherwise be ambiguous. The precedence is a number in the range 1–1200. For example, when the expression "a+b*c" is evaluated, the multiplication is done before the addition because the plus is declared internally in the Prolog system to have a higher precedence than multiplication. The precedence can be thought of as specifying how tightly binding the operator is to its arguments. The lower the precedence, the more tightly binding it is. It is also necessary to specify the associativity in situations in which the same operator (functor), or operators with the same precedence, are used more than once in an expression without brackets. In the case of infix operators it specifies whether the expression to the left of the operator should be evaluated before or after the expression on the right. This information is supplied by providing a pattern for the operator, taking one of the following forms:

fx, fy, xfx, xfy, yfx, yfy

The y indicates the expression to be evaluated first, while the x indicates that the evaluation of the expression is to be "delayed". Where the evaluation of expressions is not an issue, we can think of the precedence and associativity as providing the necessary information for translation into normal Prolog clauses. The principal functor will be the operator with the lowest precedence. For example, a+b*c translates to +(a,*(b,c)), and if + is declared as having associativity yfx then a+b+c translates into +(+(a,b),c).

Some simple examples of the use of **op** are:

```
?- op(40, fx, with).
yes
?- assert(with tom).
yes
?- with X.
X = tom
yes
?- op(60, xfy, and).
yes
?- assert(beer and skittles).
yes
?- X and Y.
X = beer
Y = skittles
yes
```

You may find it useful to declare the editing predicate that we defined earlier, **edit**, as prefix. This will avoid the need to provide brackets around the file name. For example:

```
?- op(40, fx, edit).

?- edit example.
```

You will need to change the definition of **edit** to use prefix notation.

4.8 Type checking

In the previous chapter the rules for "spaces" and "fact" had a check on the argument of the form "N > 0" to ensure that a legal value was being passed. If the rules were to be passed a term that was not a number, this would cause an exception to be raised (Prolog would produce an error message) at run time that would inform us of the type clash. This is very useful when debugging our programs, but it is often much more desirable to check that arguments are what they should be within the code. There are several built-in predicates that do this which are summarized in the following table:

Built-in	Succeeds when argument is:
isvar/1	variable
nonvar/1	not a variable
atom/1	atom
integer/1	integer
real/1	floating point
number/1	integer or float

We can use these predicates to validate arguments, and where they cannot be validated we can either silently fail or use an additional clause to write an error message. They all take a single argument that is indicated by the /1.

4.9 Comparing terms

We have already seen how arithmetical expressions can be compared with the usual operators >, <, >=, =<. It is also possible to compare any two terms. There is a standard ordering for terms in that variables come before numbers, which come before atoms, which come before compound terms. Older variables come before newer ones. Numbers are treated in numeric order; where there is an integer and float of the same value the integer comes first. Atoms are in alphabetical order. Compound terms are principally ordered by their number of arguments. Where two compound structures have the same number of arguments the ordering is by the principal functor and then by the arguments. The available operators for comparing terms are: @<, @=<, @> and @>=. Examples are:

```
? - X @< 46.
yes
?- 46 @< tree.
yes
?- tree @< tred.
no
?- tree @< a(X).
yes
?- a(X) @< a(f).
yes
?- a(X) @< a(X,f).
yes
```

Exercises 4

1. A last in first out stack (often called a LIFO stack) is a data structure that allows us two basic operations: **push** and **pop**. We use **push** to put a new element on the top of the stack. We use **pop** to remove the top element from the stack. Elements belonging to the stack can be represented in Prolog by using facts with the functor stack. Show how **push** and **pop** can be implemented in Prolog, using **asserta** and retract, by defining rules for **push** and **pop**. This is an example of their use:

```
?- push(item1).
?- push(item2).
?- push(item3).
?- pop(X).
X = item3
?- pop(X).
X = item2
```

2. Define a rule that will give the current size of the stack being used in question 1. This will need to use the **count** rule to count the number of stacked entries in the database

3. Define a rule that will clear the current stack. This will best be implemented using the built-in predicate **abolish**.

4. Add a subgoal to the factorial rule that checks that the argument is an integer and add a clause that produces an error message if the argument is not an integer.

CHAPTER FIVE
Structures

5.1 Matching variables with structures

The data structures of Prolog are called terms and comprise a functor and
a number of components, which may be simple constants and variables as
we have met already and collections of these items. The simplest kind of
structure is of the form **falcon(kestrel)**, where **falcon** is the functor of
the structure and the constant **kestrel** is its single component. We can
think of this as a record called **falcon** with one field. Structures can have
more than one component, or field, as we have already found out, but
structures can also have structures occurring as components, such as:

    car(body, engine(pistons,crank))

The depth of the nesting of structures within each other is virtually un-
limited. Car is a structure of arity 2. A single structure comprises its
functor, its opening bracket and all the components up to the corresponding closing bracket.

The pattern matching technique, *unification*, will allow variables to be
matched not only with constants but with any structure. To see how this
works enter the following fact into Prolog's database:

    car(body, engine(fuel_system,electrics(battery,starter,lights))).

We can think of this as a record describing the hierarchical relationship
between some components of a car. If it helps, think of it as a tree, with the
functor as its root.

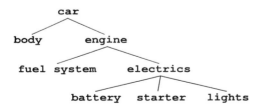

We can now query the car database containing this one fact:

```
?- car(X, Y).
X = body
Y = engine(fuel_system,electrics(battery, starter, lights))
```

Here Y has become instantiated to the entire structure having the functor **engine**. It is very important to understand that a variable can match any structure at all, regardless of how complicated the structure is.

In much the same way, a structure occurring in a query can match a structure occurring in the head of a rule. For example, we might have a rule for calculating the tax payable given a structure of the form **salary(Gross,Taxrate)**:

```
get_tax(salary(Gross,Taxrate), Tax):-
    Tax is Gross * Taxrate.
```

This can then be queried with:

```
?- get_tax(salary(12000,0.25), X).
X = 3000.0
```

5.2 Matching structures with structures

Consider the query:

```
?- car(_,engine(X,Y)).
```

taken with our second example concerning the car engine. Here we are trying to match the structure **engine(X,Y)**, which occurs in the query, with the structure

```
engine(fuel_system,electrics(battery,starter,lights))
```

which occurs in the fact. As you might expect, this succeeds, with X matching

```
fuel_system
```

and Y matching the structure

```
electrics(battery,starter,lights)
```

So the answer to the query is:

```
X = fuel_system
Y = electrics(battery,starter,lights)
```

We might say we have picked out the two components of an engine.

We can go as deep as we like into the structure in order to pick out the components that interest us. For example:

```
?- car(_, engine(_,electrics(Z,W,Q))).
Z = battery
W = starter
```

```
Q = lights
```

Notice that when we are trying to match two structures they can only be matched, or unified, if they have the same functor and their components can be matched. We cannot use a variable in place of the functor name, and therefore cannot make queries of the following type:

```
?- car(W, X(Y,Z)).
```

Exercises 5a

1. What are the arities of the following structures:
   (a) `f(g(h(i)))`
   (b) `cord(Y, Y,ab(X))`
   (c) `X is 6 + 19`
2. Give the instantiations that occur when the following pairs of structures are unified, i.e. give the complete component that each variable becomes instantiated to:
   (a) `bicycle(frame, wheels(spokes,hub),handlebar)`
       with:
       `bicycle(X, Y, Z)`
   (b) `document(preface, Y, chapter(Z), index)`
       with:
       `document(X, contents, chapter(section(paragraph)), index)`

5.3 Examining and building structures

Structures can be examined and manipulated using the predicates `functor(T,F,A)` and `arg(N,Term,A)`. A goal `functor(Term,Functor, Arity)` will be true if `Functor` is the functor of term `Term`, and `Arity` is its arity, thus:

```
?- functor(electrics(battery,starter,lights), F, A).
F = electrics
A = 3
?- functor(Term, electrics, 3).
Term = electrics(_28102,_28103,_28103).
```

In the first example, Prolog is passed a simple structure and returns its functor and arity. In the second example, it constructs a "general" term with the functor `electrics` and three uninstantiated variables as its components.

A goal `arg(N,Term,Comp)` will be true if component `Comp` is the Nth component of term `Term`, thus:

```
?- arg(2, electrics(battery,starter,lights), Comp).
```

```
Comp = starter
?- functor(Term, electrics, 3),
   arg(1, Term, battery),
   arg(2, Term, starter),
   arg(3, Term, lights).
Term = electrics(battery,starter,lights)
```

In the first example we ask Prolog for the second component, **Comp**, of the electrics structure. In the second example, we use **functor** to construct a term with functor **electrics** and with three uninstantiated variables as components, then use **arg** to instantiate these components.

5.4 Searching trees

A commonly used data structure in computer science is the *tree*. It is used to store information in a particularly ordered fashion to facilitate the connections (relationships) between various parts of the data. Many things in the natural and scientific world form tree structures. We also find tree structures in human affairs, for example a management structure.

We can define a tree in terms of its nodes. The nodes are the parts where the information is kept. For the management example, a node would probably contain the name of the person and his or her subordinates. For the sake of simplicity we are going to limit our discussion to what are known as binary trees. A general type of tree could have any number of branches from a node leading to other nodes, whereas a binary tree always has exactly two. Thus, each of our management tree records, or terms, will be a structure containing two components, the first being a constant (the person's name) and the second a structure with two components (as we are limiting ourselves to a binary tree): the names of the two people managed. The node right at the top of the tree (computer scientists and genealogists always imagine trees to grow downwards) is known as the "root node". For our management example the root node is:

```
management_tree(adams, manages(brown,collins)).
```

The facts for **brown** and **collins** are:

```
management_tree(brown, manages(dorking,evans)).
management_tree(collins, manages(fortnum,gault)).
```

To keep this example to a manageable size, we will end our tree with facts for **dorking, evans, fortnum** and **gault**. These introduce **null**, which stands for "no one".

```
management_tree(dorking, manages(null,null)).
management_tree(evans, manages(null,null)).
management_tree(fortnum, manages(null,null)).
management_tree(gault, manages(null,null)).
```

Here is our management database in "binary tree" form:

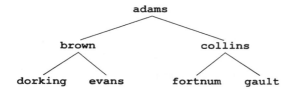

We can write a Prolog rule to navigate through the tree structure in various ways. One way is known as preorder. In this case we start at the root and list the left "manages" node and then the left "manages" node of that "manages", until we reach null, when we list the right "manages" and then the right "manages" of the parent and so on. It is a left to right, depth-first method of listing nodes. It is succinctly described as the root node followed by the left "manages" node in preorder followed by the right "manages" node in preorder. This translates wonderfully easily into Prolog (we must include the boundary case as the first clause):

```
preorder(null).
preorder(Name):-
management_tree(Name, manages(NameS1,NameS2)),
    writeln(Name),
    preorder(NameS1),
    preorder(NameS2).
```

In response to the query:

```
?- preorder(adams).
```

Prolog will give us:

```
adams
brown
dorking
evans
collins
fortnum
gault
yes
```

Here is the first part of the solution tree for this query. This is a good example to use for drawing a solution tree as it is quite complex, but try to envisage this as a mechanical process. Start with the query at the top and write the match with the head of a rule underneath; note the instantiations in curly brackets. Then proceed left to right through the subgoals remembering to make the necessary substitutions for the variables that have become instantiated. When the subgoals for a clause have been written, take the leftmost subgoal and complete its solution tree before moving on

51

to the next subgoal. It is then just a matter of repeating the process for each subgoal.

I have shortened some of the symbols in the tree for space reasons:

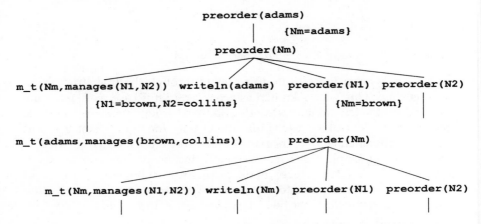

The unconnected lines show where the tree has not been completed. Try to complete this tree on paper. Note that, where **adams** is written and the next goal to be solved is **preorder(N1)**, **N1** is instantiated to **brown** because of the unification of the first subgoal **m_t(Nm, manages(N1,N2))** with the ground clause.

Exercises 5b

1. For the following structure, name all the functors and components.

    sentence(noun_phrase(adjective,noun), verb_phrase).

2. A single-user computer can be represented by a structure having the following fields: cpu, which is a structure containing components for make and model; memory; disk, which is a structure containing components for type of disk (floppy or hard) and capacity; finally, there is a component for the monitor type, which is a structure with components for the resolution and monochrome/colour indicator. Write several facts in Prolog that conform to this structure. Using a query that uses **assertz**, create new facts corresponding to that part of the structure that concerns the disk.

3. A postorder listing may be achieved by taking a node and listing the left "manages" in postorder and then the right "manages" in postorder followed by the node itself. Define a rule "postorder" that will list any part of the management structure given at the end of this chapter in postorder.

4. Add a parameter to the preorder or postorder rule that serves to indi-

cate the depth within the management tree. Use this to obtain an indented version of the management tree. i.e. your output for:

```
?- preorder(adams).
```

should look like:

```
adams
    brown
        dorking
        evans
    collins
        fortnum
        gault
    yes
```

CHAPTER SIX

Lists

6.1 Defining a list

A very useful data structure in Prolog is the list. In fact it is just a structure, but it has been given a syntax that makes it particularly easy to use. Lists in Prolog are very much what we commonly understand by lists in normal use. If you have used Lisp then you will be familiar with the idea already. Also, a singly linked list as might be defined in a conventional language is much the same. Any list in Prolog is surrounded by square brackets, and the individual entries of the list are separated by commas. Here is a list of towns as it might be written in Prolog:

`[coventry,leeds,bradford,rugby,sheffield]`

However, we cannot enter such a list into Prolog's database without it having a functor, such as:

`towns([coventry,leeds,bradford,rugby,sheffield]).`

Enter it into the database and make the following query:

`?- towns(X).`

The interpreter will respond with the list `[coventry, etc.]` that has been associated with the functor `towns`. Only a variable or another list can match with a list. A list may consist of a single element, as in:

`towns([sheffield]).`

or no elements at all:

`towns([]).`

`[]` is called the empty list or sometimes the null list.

6.2 Heads and tails

To get at individual components of a list we have a convention that lets us distinguish the first element(s) of a list from the remaining list: this is achieved by the character |, which you will normally find on the far right- or left-hand side of your keyboard. To see how this works, type the following queries:

```
?- towns([X|Y]).
?- towns([X,Y|Z]).
```

The response to the first query will be:

```
X = coventry
Y = [leeds,bradford,rugby,sheffield]
```

The response to the second query will be:

```
X = coventry
Y = leeds
Z = [bradford,rugby,sheffield]
```

What the | does is to make what occurs on the left of it become instantiated to the head or first element(s) of the list and what is on the right of the | to become instantiated to the tail or remainder of the list, which is itself a list. So, if you type the following you will get all of the list except **coventry**:

```
?- towns([_|Y]).
```

Note that, because the tail of a list is itself a list, whatever is on the right-hand side of the |, if it is not a variable, must use list notation. Or, put another way, what is on the right of the | must be capable of matching with a list, i.e. it must be either a variable or a list. The following query will therefore produce a syntax error:

```
?- towns([X|Y,Z]).
```

Note

Most errors made by the newcomer to list processing (whether using Prolog or Lisp) are a result of not distinguishing between a list (or the tail of a list) and an element of a list. Take great care to make this distinction and you will save yourself a great deal of trouble.

If we want the second element of a list we could write:

```
?- towns([_|[Y|_]]).
```

This works because the tail of a list is also a list, and so can be treated in the same way as the first list, i.e. it can be broken into its head and tail using the **[H|T]** construct. This does not look like a very nice way of getting the nth element of a list, but it is easy to define a predicate that will do it for us using only what we know already. Specifically, we would like to define a predicate to write the Nth element of a list, given the list and the number N of the element.

We start by defining the "boundary case", that is how we get the first element:

```
getnth([X|_], 1) :-
    writeln(X).
```

This will clearly write the first element of a list. Now we try to define the general case so that it will naturally work backwards to the case we have just defined, in much the same way as the factorial function did, thus:

```
getnth([X|Y], N) :-
    N > 1,
    N1 is N - 1,
    getnth(Y, N1).
```

This recursively discards the head of the list N – 1 times, at which point the first clause is called because of the match with the number 1. To see how this works it is easier to consider a concrete example. Take the query:

```
?- getnth([coventry,leeds,bradford,rugby], 3)
```

and manually trace its execution like this:

1. Query matches on second clause, with X = [coventry, Y = leeds, bradford, rugby], N = 3.
2. **N > 1** succeeds.
3. **N1 is N** – 1 instantiates N1 to 2.
4. **getnth([leeds,bradford,rugby],2)** is called.
5. Query matches on second clause, with X = leeds, Y = [bradford, rugby], N = 2.
6. **N > 1** succeeds;
7. **N1 is N - 1** instantiates N1 to 1.
8. **(getnth([bradford,rugby],1)** is called.
9. Query matches on first clause, with X = bradford.
10. The only subgoal **writeln(X)** is executed causing "bradford" to be written.

If you still do not understand how this definition works for any number N, then use it on a list for different values of N with **trace** on. It is very important that you should be able to hand-trace the execution of a goal in the above manner using pen and paper.

The rule **getnth** is recursive, as are nearly all rules that process lists. This should not be surprising, as a list is a data structure that can be defined recursively as being either the empty list or an element followed by a list.

6.3 member and append

Consider the problem of determining whether an element is a member of a list. First we see if the element is the head of the list: if it is we have finished. If it is not then we check to see if it is in the tail of the list. This is expressed very naturally in Prolog as:

```
member(X, [X|_]). /* if X is head of list then
    goal is satisfied... */
member(X, [_|Y]) :-
    member(X, Y). /* ...else look in tail */
```

The following query will produce the answer **yes**:

```
?- member(dog, [cat,dog]).
```

This is the solution tree:

```
?- member(dog,[cat,dog])
        |        {X = dog, Y = [dog]}
    member(X, [_|Y])
        |
    member(dog, [dog])
        |        {X = dog}
    member(X, [X|_])
```

If you still do not understand how it works, use the **trace** predicate to follow it in action.

Now consider a predicate that appends two lists (remember that the notation [] is used for the empty list, which has no members, and therefore neither head nor tail). An example of **append** in use is:

```
?- append([art,history], [physics,maths],L).

L = [art,history,physics,maths]
```

Note that the first list is appended to the front of the second list. This is the way **append** has always been defined in Prolog. This is the Prolog for **append**:

```
append([], L, L).
append([H|T], L, [H|U]) :-
    append(T, L, U).
```

This is rather more subtle than the previous examples and should be studied carefully. Do not be put off by how obscure this looks. The list notation is very concise, and used in such a declarative context as Prolog may make this appear unreadable to the newcomer. Within a little time this kind of statement will become familiar and readily understandable. If you can understand **append**, then you have probably grasped the most difficult concept in Prolog, so be prepared to take some time over understanding it.

The first clause should be readily understood: the empty list appended to any list produces the same list. The second clause can be read declaratively as: If the list we are appending has head H and tail T and we append this to L then the resulting list will have H as the head, and the tail of the list, U, will be the result of appending the tail of the first list, T, to the second list, L. Or, put another way, the second clause can be described by: The resulting list must have the same head as the first list. The resulting list's tail must be the result of appending the tail of the first list with all of the second list.

6.4 A method for defining rules that manipulate lists

When you are defining rules that manipulate lists, it is a useful tip always to break the lists into their heads and tails in the head of the rule, identify which heads correspond, and then form the necessary relationships between the lists' heads and tails in the body of the rule. This is for the general part of the rule. The boundary condition is usually very straightforward and can nearly always be written down straightaway. This may be summarized by the following steps:

1. Express all the lists in the head of the rule as having a head and a tail.
2. Give the same name to those heads of the list that must be the same.
3. Give the same name to those tails of the list that must be the same.
4. Form the necessary relationships between the remaining heads and tails in the body of the rule.
5. Simplify any head and tail pairs that do not need to be expressed as both head and tail.

We may see how this works by returning to the **append** predicate. Following the first instruction we express the head of the rule as:

```
append([H1|T1], [H2|T2], [H3|T3]):-
```

Using step 2, it should be clear that the resulting list must start with the same element as the first list, giving:

```
append([H|T1],[H2|T2],[H|T3]):-
```

There does not seem to be much more we can do with step 2, so we try step 3. This does not help, so we move on to step 4. Now it should be clear that T3 must be the result of appending T1 to [H2 | T2], so the rule is:

```
append([H|T1], [H2|T2], [H|T3]):-
    append(T1, [H2|T2], T3).
```

The last step is now used to replace [H2 | T2] with a single variable as there is no need for this list to be separated out into a head and a tail. So finally our rule (without the boundary case) is:

```
append([H|T1], L, [H|T3]):-
    append(T1, L, T3).
```

Which is equivalent to the version given above.

6.5 Which is input, which is output?

One feature of Prolog worth bearing in mind is that when we define predicates to perform various tasks on lists or structures we are only specifying relationships – we are not saying this variable is the input and another variable is the output. That is only the way we think about it. Prolog has no such concept of input and output parameters. This means that predicates will "work backwards". If we input the definition for member and then the following query, using ; (or the **Another solution** dialogue) to get all the solutions:

```
?- member(X, [shoes,ships,sealing_wax,cabbages]).
X = shoes;
X = ships;
X = sealing_wax;
X = cabbages;
no
```

we get what at first seems a remarkable result but on closer examination is an inevitable consequence of Prolog. It is very important to remember that we are constantly thinking about Prolog in a conventional and procedural manner and it will often surprise us because of its greater power.

We get a similar result if we use **append** with the third parameter instantiated and variables as the first two parameters:

```
?- append(X, Y, [a,b,c,d]).
X = []
Y = [a,b,c,d];
X = [a]
Y = [b,c,d];
X = [a,b]
Y = [c,d];
X = [a,b,c]
Y = [d];
X = [a,b,c,d]
Y = [];
no
```

This feature is not just a novelty but can be very beneficial. Consider the case that you are processing some list a part at a time. The parts that you want to process separately are divided by a certain key value. In the case of a string of characters represented by their ASCII codes this key value might be 32 for the space character. The space usually divides words, so you can use this to enable you to process one word at a time. How do you pick out each part of the list up to the next space? It is very simple using **append**. Here is a rule that returns the next word from the ASCII list and the rest of the list that has yet to be processed:

```
process_sentence(Word, Listin, Listout):-
    append(Word, [32], L),
    append(L, Listout, Listin).
```

Here each word is returned as a list of its ASCII codes. For example:

```
?- process_sentence(Word, [76, 79, 79, 75, 32, 65, 72,
69, 65, 68], L).
gives:
Word = [76,79,79,75]
L = [65,72,69,65,68]
```

The rule can be simplified by combining the two appends:

```
process_sentence(Word, Listin, Listout):-
    append(Word, [32|Listout], Listin).
```

6.6 Sorting

How might we sort a list of integers into ascending order? We want a predicate of the form **sort(Unsorted,Sorted)**. We can start by defining the boundary case: a list consisting of a single element is sorted:

```
sort([X], [X]).
```

We now have to pick off the remaining cases. There are many different ways of sorting a list. This method is based on the "bubble sort", which basically consists in examining the first two elements of a list, reordering them if necessary, sorting the remainder of the list, and then seeing if the start of the ordered part is greater or less than the greater of the first two considered.

```
sort([H1,H2|T], [H1,H3|T3]):-
    (H1 =< H2),
    sort([H2|T], [H3|T3]),
    (H1 =< H3).
```

Here we check that the first element, H1, is less than the second, H2, so they are in order, then sort the remainder. If the head of this, H3, is greater or equal to H1 then the output list must be H1 followed by the sorted list H3 | T3.

```
sort([H1,H2|T], [H3|S]):-
```

```
    (H1 =< H2),
    sort([H2|T], [H3|T3]),
    (H1 > H3),
    sort([H1|T3], S).
```

This is the same as the previous case only H1 is greater than H3. Next we have:

```
sort([H1,H2|T], [H3|S]):-
    (H1 > H2),
    sort([H1|T], [H3|T3]),
    (H2 > H3),
    sort([H2|T3], S).
```

This time the first element of the input list is greater than the second. We basically repeat the last two clauses taking account of this. The final clause is therefore:

```
sort([H1,H2|T], [H2,H3|T3]):-
    (H1 > H2),
    sort([H1|T], [H3|T3]),
    (H2 =< H3).
```

Note that the sort as it has been defined is only suitable for sorting numbers. We have made the sort rather inflexible as to the types of thing it can sort. It is common not to build the actual test that the sort depends on directly into the sorting rule. We often find it convenient to define a predicate such as **gt(X,Y)** that we can define independently of the sort. A typical definition might be:

```
gt(X,Y) :- X > Y.
```

Which we might use in the example above. We might prefer to define it using the standard ordering comparison:

```
gt(X,Y) :- X @> Y.
```

This enables the sort to be used on a much wider range of types. Our sort, using **gt**, becomes:

```
sort([X], [X]).
sort([H1,H2|T], [H1,H3|T3]):-
    gt(H2, H1),
    sort([H2|T], [H3|T3]),
    gt(H3, H1).
sort([H1,H2|T], [H3|S]):-
    gt(H2, H1),
    sort([H2|T], [H3|T3]),
    gt(H1, H3),
    sort([H1|T3], S).
```

```
sort([H1,H2|T], [H3|S]):-
    gt(H1, H2),
    sort([H1|T], [H3|T3]),
    gt(H2, H3),
    sort([H2|T3], S).
sort([H1,H2|T], [H2,H3|T3]):-
    gt(H1, H2),
    sort([H1|T], [H3|T3]),
    gt(H3, H2).
```

This is a far more convenient form because we can change the definition of **gt(X, Y)** without looking at the sort code. It can now be generalized to sort anything we like. Later in the chapter we will use it to sort cells on a spreadsheet.

The above version of bubble sort was rather unsubtle: we broke the problem down into a list of cases and dealt with each in turn. An alternative and much more elegant approach is to define a predicate, **swap(L1,L2)**, that takes a list and swaps the first pair of elements that are out of order. It fails if all pairs are in order. This can be defined as:

```
swap([X,Y|Rest], [Y,X|Rest]):-
    gt(X, Y).
swap([H|T], [H|Rest]):-
    swap(T, Rest).
```

The first clause swaps the first pair if they are out of order. The second clause recurses on the tail, leaving the head of the list in place.

The bubble sort can then easily be defined by using **swap(X,Y)** until it fails, at which point we know that the list must be sorted:

```
bubblesort(List, Sorted):-
    swap(List, Part_sorted),
    bubblesort(Part_sorted, Sorted).
bubblesort(L, L).
```

This can most easily be understood by thinking about what it does to a few simple lists. For example, what does it do to these lists?

```
[1,2,3,4]
[5,1,2,3]
[1,2,3,5]
```

6.7 Lists containing structures

The elements of a list may be atoms, structures, variables or any other terms, including other lists. Here is an example of a list containing other lists as its members:

```
couples([[george,pam],[bruce,sheila],[mike,jenny]]).
```

This is a list of three elements, each of which is a list containing two elements, each of which is an atom. The query:

```
?- couples([H|T]).
```

produces:

```
H = [george,pam]
T = [[bruce,sheila],[mike,jenny]]
yes
```

Consider:

```
bits([a,[b,c,d],e,[f,[g,h]]]).
```

This is a list of four elements. The first is an atom, the second is a list of three atoms, the third is an atom and the last is a list of two elements, the first of which is an atom and the second a list of two atoms.

It may come as no surprise that any structure can be an element of a list. A list itself is just another structure with a particularly simple syntax. A list is really a structure of the following form:

```
[a,b,c] = list(a,list(b,list(c,[])))
```

Obviously the left form is a lot more convenient, but in all respects, other than the way you and the Prolog system write it, it is as although it was declared in the right-hand fashion. The infix symbol | can be thought of as the list functor rather than the word 'list' I have used above. Then if we think of a list expressed in a prefix form rather than infix it would be:

```
|(a,|(b,|(c,[])))
```

This way of thinking or writing a list can be very useful when considering unification. Consider the above list being unified with:

```
|(H,T).
```

It's rather obvious that H is unified with "a" and T is unified with the structure immediately following the "a", which is itself a list. Remember that the form of a list as it is normally written is really only syntactic sugar, something that makes writing and reading lists more convenient; the actual structure of a list is as shown above, which explains its behaviour when unified with other list structures.

A simple application of using structures within a list is the following, in which we imagine that we are implementing a spreadsheet program in Prolog. A spreadsheet consists of an array of cells. Some of the cells have values that we display from time to time as the spreadsheet is updated. As a great many of the cells do not have a value, it is efficient to keep a list of only those cells that have values. Many parts of the spreadsheet program will want access to the spreadsheet's values, so we may feel justified in storing the values as an asserted fact containing the list. The cells are labelled by their row position (1, 2, 3, . . .) and by their column position (a, b, c, . . .). The fact containing the list to store the cell values could be:

```
cell_values([cell(1,a,'CARS'), cell(4,e,6438)]).
```

A particular cell's value, if it has one, may be obtained very simply by using **member**:

```
get_value(Rownum, Colname, Value):-
    cell_values(Values),
    member(cell(Rownum,Colname,Value), Values).
```

Although the use of the functor **cell** can be obviated, its use makes the program more readable and more easily updated if requirements change. Using structures in this way is giving us the same advantage as using records in other languages. It quite literally gives us the facility to structure our data, rather than deal with long unstructured lists of characters, integers or whatever.

We might wish to store the list of cells in sorted order by ascending values of column and row. In order to do this it is only necessary to define the predicate **gt** and then use the bubble sort we defined earlier in this chapter. As we want columns to be more significant than rows, we define **gt** like this:

```
gt(cell(_,C1,_), cell(_,C2,_)):-
    C1 @> C2.
gt(cell(R1,C,_), cell(R2,C,_)):-
    R1 > R2.
```

Note that the first cell is always considered greater than the second cell if the first cell's column is greater than that of the second cell. The second clause is for when the two cells have the same column, in which case we need to test the row numbers.

Exercises 6

1. Define a list called weekdays, containing Monday, Tuesday, etc.
2. Given that the first of the month is a Monday, define a predicate to print the day for any date in a month.
3. Define a predicate **delete(X, L1, L2)** that removes the element X from the list L1 to yield the list L2.
4. Define a predicate to find the last element in a list.
5. Write a rule that gives the intersection of two sets represented as lists.
6. Write a rule to give the union of two sets represented as lists. There must not be any repeated elements.
7. Define a predicate **reverse(X, Y)** that reverses the order of the elements of X and instantiates the resulting list to Y. Hint – use **append**.
8. Define a rule to sort the cells of the spreadsheet into ascending order by Rownum.
9. Hand trace the solution to the query:
   ```
   ?- member(X,[tom,dick]),write(X),fail.
   ```

65

10. A list of the prices of items in stock is kept as a clause in the form:

    `stock([item(1023,99.95),item(1024,29.95),item(1021,46.75),...]).`

    Each member of the list is a structure giving the item number and its price. Write a rule, `stock_price(Num,Price)`, that expects to be given the item number and returns its price.

11. For the stock items in the above question, write a `gt` predicate that would allow the list of stock to be bubble sorted by item number.

CHAPTER SEVEN
Program control

This chapter introduces Prolog features that affect the flow of control of a program that includes **cut**, perhaps the most infamous feature of Prolog, which is often likened to **goto** in other languages for its lack of readability. Some Prolog efficiency issues concerning clause selection via indexing and some of the ramifications of Prolog's execution model are discussed.

7.1 Or

As well as being able to specify rules where to satisfy a goal one first satisfies one goal and then goes on to satisfy another goal, it is possible to say "To satisfy a goal solve the first subgoal or solve the second". As long as one or other subgoal succeeds, then the main goal will succeed. The symbol for **or** is **;**. For example:

```
happy(X):-
    rich(X) ; lucky(X).
```

meaning someone is happy if they are either rich or lucky. If the database contains the following facts:

```
rich(tom).
lucky(dick).
```

the following may then be produced:

```
?- happy(X).
X = tom;
X = dick
```

In fact, the **or** construct is not strictly necessary. We could have expressed the above rule without using an "or":

```
happy(X):-
    rich(X).
happy(X):-
    lucky(X).
```

This is exactly equivalent to the previous definition. The **or** is included for convenience where the second construct seems heavy-handed.

When using "or" in everyday language we often use it to mean that only one of the alternatives is true, as in "It is either too hot or too cold". In Prolog **goal1 ; goal2** means that **goal1** can be satisfied or **goal2** can be satisfied. In logic, **or** is commonly called *logical disjunction* and is often represented as a large V.

In procedural terms, when the **or** is encountered by the interpreter it creates a backtrack point consisting of the second part of the **or**, and then attempts to satisfy the first part of the **or**, failing which it will backtrack to and try to satisfy the second part.

7.2 Cut

cut is a special control facility in Prolog that enables the programmer to restrict the backtracking options open to the Prolog system as it executes a goal. The symbol for **cut** is **!**, and it appears as a subgoal on the right-hand side, i.e. in the body, of a rule. The first part of this section will explain the workings of **cut** quite informally and then we will examine the procedural semantics of **cut** in rather more depth.

The interpreter, on meeting **cut** for the first time, will let it succeed, but any subsequent failure will cause the interpreter to backtrack to the last backtrack point of the parent goal. This can save the interpreter a lot of pointless searching, and it is more economical on memory because the interpreter will be remembering fewer backtrack points. In this respect, **cut** is a very pragmatic feature of Prolog as it allows us to use our knowledge about a particular situation to guide the Prolog system away from pointless searching. Consider the following:

```
mammal(X):-
    warm_blooded(X),
    !,
    four_legs(X).

warm_blooded(cat).
warm_blooded(dog).
four_legs(cat).
four_legs(dog).
```

If we make the query:

```
?- mammal(X).
```

we get the response:

```
X = cat;
no
```

as the only solution: "dog" does not appear as a solution when we ask for a second solution by entering a semicolon (or via the **Another solution** dialogue). Backtracking has jumped over the possibility of resatisfying **warm_blooded** because the cut has removed the choice point of **warm_blooded** that was created when **warm_blooded(X)** was matched with **warm_blooded(cat)**.

This is not a very realistic example as we would normally want **warm_blooded** to be resatisfied. In the case where we are looking up a value, and we are only interested in one such value, we can prevent backtracking occurring. As an example consider part of the **cars** database:

```
supplier(ford,uk,'21 Tinsgate, Dagenham','01 233 4821').
supplier(blmc,uk,'18 Beadle Road, Cowley','0325 24122').
supplier(fiat,italy,'333 Via Alphonse, Turin','0101 888⌐
376 3983').
```

We might require a single address for each manufacturer, even if there was more than one address given. It may be our requirement that we only mail one address for each manufacturer. Here we would use **cut** like this:

```
process_supplier(Supplier):-
    get_address(Supplier,Address),
    mail(Supplier,Address).
get_address(Supplier,Address):-
    supplier(Supplier,Country,Address1,_),
    !,
    string_concat(Address1,Country,Address).
```

The predicate **string_concat** is to be taken as defined elsewhere.

On satisfying **get_address, supplier** is first satisfied, and if it is possible for it to be resatisfied then a backtrack point is created. The cut is then executed, and this removes any backtrack points created since entering the current goal, so preventing any possible future backtracking to the **supplier** subgoal.

The effect of **cut** is in fact rather more far-reaching than has so far been implied. Not only does it remove any choice points that have been created within the clause where it is activated, it also removes any choice points that the parent goal may have. This simple example establishes whether there is an electrical fault in a given electrical component:

```
electrical_fault(X):-
    capacitor(X),
    !,
    impedance(X,R),
    R < 5000.
electrical_fault(X):-
    fuse(X),
    !,
    impedance(X,R),
    R > 100.
fuse(f436).
impedance(f436, 200).
capacitor(c782).
impedance(c782, 1000).
```

We might normally expect the goal **electrical_fault** to be called with a known component as in:

```
?- electrical_fault(f436).
```

The first clause for **electrical_fault** would have failed at the **capacitor(f436)** goal and backtracking would allow the second clause to be used. Note that the **capacitor(f436)** goal failed *before* the cut could be executed, which means that the backtrack point for **electrical_fault** is left intact.

However, if we make the query:

```
?- electrical_fault(X)
```

we get the response:

```
X = c782;

no
```

with no more solutions obtainable by entering a semicolon. Exactly as before, the backtrack point created for **electrical_fault** when

```
electrical_fault(X)
```

is matched against its first clause has been removed owing to the cut. This prevents **f436** appearing as a solution.

From a programming point of view we can justify the use of the cut in the above example by the simple observation that when

```
electrical_fault
```

is called we expect its argument to be instantiated. Therefore, once we have established that the component in question is a capacitor or a fuse or whatever, we know that there is no point in trying to match it with another component. Therefore it is expedient to prevent any unnecessary searching by including the cut immediately after we have established what we are dealing with. It should be clear that the declarative semantics has been changed somewhat. We no longer have the luxury of calling the

`electrical_fault`

goal with a variable and achieving a complete result.

Use of **cut** forces us to think hard about the procedural semantics of Prolog, i.e. about what actually happens when the query is being solved. This is because the cut affects the choice points that are available *at the point* that it is executed. The following example is rather more abstract than usual, but it is being used to convey the precise semantics of the cut.

Consider the following partial solution tree corresponding to the clauses

```
a:- b, c, d.
b:- e, !, f.
b:- g, h.
f:- i.
f:- j.
i.
j.
```

This is the solution tree for the query ?- **a.**

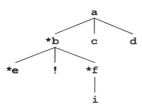

Choice points have been marked with *. In order to understand the exact procedural semantics we are going to follow the execution of the goals in great detail.

- The call to **a** immediately causes a call to **b**.
- At the point when the body of **b** is being executed there is a choice point available for **b** (hence the asterisk).
- The next goal to be executed is **e**. When **e** is executed it also leaves a choice point.
- Now the cut is executed, which removes the choice point for both **e** and **b**. It is important to realize that if **cut** is executed at precisely this point then it removes the choice points within its scope.
- Execution now proceeds with **f**, which also creates a choice point. This choice point, because it comes after the cut, is left alone.
- At this point control passes to **c**.
- When **c** fails control then passes to the most recent choice point, which is at **f**.
- Execution proceeds forward again with control being passed to **c** which, of course, fails again.

- At this point the whole query fails without any further backtracking because the choice points before the call to **f** have been removed by the cut.

The entire procedural semantics of cut can be described as follows. When **cut** is executed it:

- succeeds;
- removes any choice points for the calling goal;
- removes any choice points for goals in the same clause as the *cut that exist at the time of the call.*

The final point has been emphasized because the cut does not affect the choice points of those goals that come after the cut, and this is a peculiarly undeclarative feature, making the order of subgoals extremely important.

cut enables us to program the equivalent of **IF... THEN... ELSE** type constructs found in other languages. Conventionally, only one part of an **IF... THEN... ELSE** statement is executed, in other words the clauses are *mutually exclusive*. However, in Prolog, if the first clause for a rule succeeds but a subsequent goal fails, we can go on to backtrack into the second. This is often not desirable. We can stop the backtracking by including **cut** immediately after the condition for the particular clause.

To use the spreadsheet as an example again, consider the layout of the cells on the screen. A spreadsheet screen looks something like:

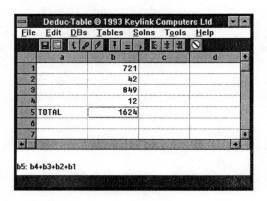

A limited number of cells only can actually be shown on the screen. The cells go from a1 up to at least z256. At any one time there is a current cell, which is the one the user can change the contents of, or perform the calculation of. In the above example this is b5. The user can change the current cell by using the cursor keys, but if the cursor is already at row 1 and the user presses the up arrow then we do not want to change anything as it is impossible to go higher up the spreadsheet. The same is true if the user presses the left arrow key when the cursor is at the column labelled "a".

In a conventional language we might express this as:

```
IF key = 'up' THEN
    IF current_row = 1 THEN
        return
    ELSE
        current_row = current_row - 1
        move_cursor(current_row)
    ENDIF
ELSEIF key = 'left' THEN
    IF current_col = 'A' THEN
        return
    ELSE
        current_col = current_col - 1
        move_cursor(current_col)
        ENDIF
    ELSEIF key = 'right' THEN
        .
        .
        .
```

We can express the same mutually exclusive clauses in Prolog by using **cut** as follows.

We first define our predicate to be:

```
process_key(Key,Current_row,Current_col,New_row,New_col)
```

We need new parameter names for the altered **Current_row** and **Current_col** because we cannot destructively assign new values to them. (97 is the ASCII code for a.)

```
process_key(up,1,Current_col,1,Current_col):-
    !.
process_key(up,Current_row,Current_col,New_row,Current_col):-
    New_row is Current_row - 1,
    move_cursor(New_row),
    !.
process_key(left,Current_row,97,Current_row,97):-
    !.
process_key(left,Current_row,Current_col,Current_row,New_col):-
    New_col is Current_col - 1,
    move_cursor(New_col),
    !.
    .
    .
```

7.3 Cut/fail – the eight queens problem

An important Prolog programming construct that involves the use of cut is the `cut/fail` combination. This is where `cut` is called immediately before a call to `fail`. We use this when we want to force a failure with no prospect of backtracking into any subsequent clauses for the rule in which `cut/fail` is placed. It is a very definite kind of failure, useful when we have entirely established that something is false. The eight queens problems has an elegant solution that shows how the `cut/fail` combination can be used to excellent effect.

This is a very old problem: How do you place eight queens on a normal chessboard so that no queen can take any other? We will solve a slight variant of this, how to place n queens on a normal chessboard. The following query:

```
?- queens(8, Solution).
```

can then be used to solve the full problem. We expect **Solution** to be instantiated to some representation of the positions of the eight queens. Queens can move horizontally, vertically and diagonally any number of spaces, so it is clearly not trivial to find a solution. However, it should be immediately clear that every queen must be in a different row. Therefore an intuitive approach is to think of placing one queen at a time at some position within each row.

We will solve the problem recursively by placing a single queen and then solving the problem for solving one queen less. We will imagine that the rows and columns are labelled 1 to 8. The boundary is very straightforward, placing no queens, i.e. the queen on row 0, returns no positions:

```
queens(0, []).
```

Now for the recursive part; this will subtract 1 from the current row and make a recursive call for the rest of the solution:

```
queens(Row, [position(Row,Col)|Rest]):-
    Row > 0,
    Last_row is Row - 1,
    queens(Last_row, Rest),
```

Notice that we are returning a list of positions. The head of the list is the position of the queen about to be placed within this goal sequence. We clearly already know the row it is going on; the rest of the goal sequence will determine the column. The tail of the list, which gives the placement of the Row – 1 queens, is found from the recursive call.

Now we need to generate a candidate position for the current row; for the moment we will just give this the name **candidate_col** and consider how it is to be coded a little late. After generating the candidate column for the queen we can test if it is placed in a position where it is safe from the queens placed by the recursive call; we will call this goal unthreatened.

Therefore the goal sequence continues with:

```
candidate_col(Col),
unthreatened(position(Row,Col),Rest).
```

If **unthreatened** fails then we will backtrack into **candidate_col** for an alternative column for the queen. Clearly, **candidate_col** needs to be able to backtrack through all eight columns. Remember what was said about **member** in the previous chapter, that we can use it with a variable for the first argument to generate all elements of a list. This makes **candidate_col** very easy to define as:

```
candidate_col(Col):-
member(Col, [1,2,3,4. .6,7,8]).
```

We can define **unthreatened** recursively by noting that a position is safe if it is safe with regard to the first queen position in the list, and is safe from the queens in the rest of the list (this is the recursive call). Therefore the code for unthreatened is:

```
unthreatened(Position, [Q|Rest]):-
    safe(Position,Q),
    unthreatened(Position,Rest).
unthreatened(Position,[]).
```

Now it only remains to code **safe**. It is much easier to code what is unsafe because this is so easily defined. A queen is not safe when it is on the same horizontal, vertical, or diagonal line as another queen. If we test for each of these conditions we can then force failure by using **fail**. Unfortunately, this would not be enough. If the first clause tested whether the queens were on the same row, and the second clause tested whether they were on the same column, a failure at the first clause would cause backtracking into the second, which might then succeed. What we want is to fail and not allow the possibility of backtracking. We achieve this with the **cut/fail** goal sequence.

```
safe(position(R,_), position(R,_)):- !,fail.
safe(position(_,C), position(_,C)):- !,fail.
safe(position(R1,C1), position(R2,C2)):-
    diff(C1,C2,W),
    diff(R1,R2,H),
    H=W,!,fail.
safe(_, _). /* otherwise safe */
```

We check whether the queens are on the same diagonal by calculating the difference in rows and columns of the two queens. Notice the final clause: if none of the previous clauses are executed completely then the queen is safe, none of the cuts will have been executed and the goal will be satisfied by backtracking into the final clause.

Calculating this difference is straightforward we just have to take care to make the difference positive:

```
diff(X, Y, D):-
    X < Y,
    D is Y - X.
diff(X, Y, D):-
    X >= Y,
    D is X - Y.
```

7.4 Repeat

This built-in predicate (BIP) always succeeds and always creates a backtrack point. It behaves exactly as if it were defined by:

```
repeat.
repeat:- repeat.
```

A procedural way of interpreting this is: every time repeat is called, it is immediately satisfied and creates a backtrack point that is a call to itself.

This enables us to force goals to be repeated until they succeed. A simple example is where we require a digit (0–9) from the user. We do not want to fail if the user gets it wrong, but rather to allow retries until one is given. A Prolog rule that will only succeed when given a digit and will not fail in any event is:

```
get_digit(X):-
    repeat,
    get0(X1),
    X1 >= 48,
    X1 =< 57,
    X is X1 - 48,
    !.
```

get0(X) instantiates X to the ASCII code for a character typed at the keyboard. The ASCII codes for digits 0–9 are 48–57 inclusive, so, having read a character, we check whether it is in this range. If so, we then subtract the ASCII code for 0 from it to leave us with the integer value of the character. If an invalid character is entered, the use of **repeat** will cause us to backtrack to get0(X1). Where we have a valid character, the use of **cut** will then remove the backtrack point created by **repeat**.

The **repeat** predicate has other uses, such as creating potentially infinite loops for program control purposes, which is discussed in a later chapter.

7.5 Findall

A common requirement is to obtain *all* the solutions to a particular goal as a list. We can do this by defining a predicate that is commonly called **findall**. It has three arguments: the first indicates what we wish to collect a list of, the second is the goal to be solved and the final argument will become instantiated to the list of solutions.

For example, given the two facts:

```
warm_blooded(cat).
warm_blooded(dog).
```

We can collect the solutions to the goal **warm_blooded(X)** with the query:

```
?- findall(X,warm_blooded(X),L).
L = [cat,dog]
```

The first part of **findall** is a failure-driven loop that asserts all the solutions into the database; the second part collects these solutions into a list. Consider:

```
findall(X, Goal, Xlist):-
    call(Goal),
    assertz(queue(X)),
    fail;
    assertz(queue(bottom)),
    collect(Xlist).
```

Notice the use of the built-in predicate **call**, which allows us to call a Prolog goal that we do not know the name of until run time. Also notice the use of the "or", which allows us to assert a bottom of queue marker when there are no more solutions. The final goal is the one that collects the solutions. This rule is defined as:

```
collect(L):-
    retract(queue(X)),
    !,
    (X == bottom, !,L = []
    ; L = [X|Rest], collect(Rest)).
```

This recursively collects the solutions. We do not want to leave a backtrack point whenever **retract** is satisfied so we follow it with **cut**. We test for the bottom of the queue with **X == bottom**. This is a test that requires X to be instantiated to bottom and is more stringent than **X = bottom**, which would succeed when X is not instantiated. Look at the description of **==** in Chapter 14 for a full explanation. If we are at the bottom of the queue we terminate the list with the empty list, otherwise we make the solution, X, the head of the list to be returned and recursively collect the rest of the list.

7.6 Clause indexing

In earlier chapters Prolog's search strategy has been described very naively. In particular, Prolog avoids creating choice points where it knows that a subsequent search is not going to yield a match. It does this by generating code for each predicate that contains branch tables for each different first argument. So when the first argument to a predicate is known, it immediately knows what the candidate set of clauses, based on matching first arguments, is without having to perform the expensive operation of unification. How it does this need not concern us, but if you are interested Kogge (1991) describes it. This means that all predicates are effectively indexed on their first argument. This should influence how we program in order that we take advantage of this wherever necessary. If we have large collections of unit ground clauses we should arrange for the argument that we usually search on to be the first. Where we are unable to arrange this it may still be possible to take advantage of clause indexing by using an additional set of clauses whose purpose is nothing other than to improve access to some more fundamental set of clauses. For example, consider a set of employee records of the form:

```
employee(name, national_insurance_id, address)
```

We may have a requirement to look up employees' names based on their national insurance numbers and at the same time have a need to look up their national insurance numbers given their names. We could duplicate the table so that we have name as the first field in one instance of the table and national insurance as the first field in another instance. More efficiently, we can introduce a key to the employee facts, for example:

```
employee(key, name, national_insurance_id, address)
```

The key should be a unique integer value. We now need two sets of clauses to give us efficient access to the employee records, one for retrieval on name and one for retrieval on national insurance, for example entries of the form:

```
employee_name(name, key)
employee_ni(ni, key)
```

are required. We can define a rule to choose the correct set of clauses to use automatically by using the built-in predicate **nonvar/1** to identify an instantiation of the name or national insurance number:

```
employee(Name, NI, Address):-
    nonvar(Name),
    !,
    employee_name(Name, Key),
    employee(Key, Name, NI, Address).
employee(Name, NI, Address):-
```

```
    nonvar(NI),
    !,
    employee_ni(NI, Key),
    employee(Key, Name, NI, Address).
employee(Name, NI, Address):-
    employee(_, Name, NI, Address).
```

Notice that I have allowed the search to succeed when neither the name nor the national insurance number is known by defining a third clause that does not use the key.

When a predicate has only one candidate clause for a given call, we say that in this case the call is *determinate*. Clause indexing not only makes matching with a particular clause very much faster, it also means that many more calls are made determinate as the Prolog system can tell in advance whether a choice point is needed.

7.7 Garbage collection

The matching of structures within a Prolog program causes parts of the structures to be copied into Prolog's so-called heap area (sometimes called the global stack). At any given point it is usually the case that not all structures that have been copied for unification purposes will be referenced by active parts of the execution. The heap is expanded by claiming memory from the operating system. In severe cases this will cause excessive use of the heap, causing either memory to run out or paging to disk. Those parts of the heap that are not referenced are called garbage. In order to keep the heap area as free as possible, a garbage collector is used to reclaim unreferenced areas.

The standard way for such a garbage collector to work is to mark all the referenced areas of the heap by following all the active pointers, and then to compact the heap, thus freeing space at the top while at the same time rearranging any structure pointers to point to the new heap positions of the active structures. Of course, this all takes processing time.

Garbage collection for the most part is unobtrusive, but when we are trying to provide a very smooth-flowing interface with the user it can be frustrating to have this pause in the middle of what might otherwise seem to be an innocuous piece of code. We might also find garbage collections unwelcome in some time-critical areas of code. More advanced Prolog systems than the Keylink interpreter will offer some control over the timing of garbage collection; in certain situations you will find such facilities invaluable.

When trying to avoid the need for garbage collection you should note that backtracking is a situation in which the Prolog system can reclaim space by simply restoring pointers to its internal areas. It is a sort of instant garbage collect with no marking or compaction necessary. Thus, failure-driven loops can be a cheap and cheerful way to avoid the need for garbage collection.

Exercises 7

1. Define a predicate that checks that a word is correctly spelt by comparing it with a dictionary of words (a useful sample is given at the end of question 2). Then define a predicate, **near_miss**, that succeeds when the spelling of a word is a "near miss" with another word, which it returns, where a near miss is defined as being where the first three letters are the same and the lengths of the words are different by at most one letter. The rule for dealing with the words' lengths can be defined by:

   ```
   close_numbers(N, N).
     close_numbers(N, M):-
     N =< (M + 1),
     N >= (M - 1).
   ```

   You will also need to use the built-in predicate name that was introduced in Chapter 4. To remind you of its use, it has two arguments: the first argument is an atom and the second is the list of ASCII codes corresponding to the letters in the atom. For example:

   ```
   ?- name(duck, X).
   X = [100,117,99,107]
   ```

2. Now use the **near_miss** predicate to give the user all the near misses for each word entered. If you have duplicates you should consider the placement of cuts in your program. (You can use **read(X)** to read a word from the user – the word must be terminated with a full-stop.)

   ```
   word(ducal).
   word(ducat).
   word(duchess).
   word(duchesse).
   word(duchy).
   word(duck).
   word(duckling).
   word(duct).
   word(ductile).
   word(dud).
   word(dude).
   word(due).
   ```

```
word(duel).
word(duenna).
word(duet).
word(duff).
word(duffer).
word(duffle).
```

3. Modify the above program so that the definition of **near_miss** is that the two words start with the same character, they are within one character of being the same length and that half or more of the remaining characters are the same.

4. Use **findall** to collect a list of near misses as given by the goal **near_miss** in the previous question.

CHAPTER EIGHT

Input and output

8.1 put

As well as the **write** and **nl** predicates for output there is also **put(X)** – this has one parameter that should be instantiated to an integer value. The value should be an ASCII code representing a printable character. When executed, **put(X)** outputs the corresponding character to the current output stream (normally the screen). For example:

```
?- put(104),put(101),put(108),put(108),put(111).
```

will print "hello" on the screen. On the PC you can output any of the IBM's graphics characters as well. For example ?- **put(182).** will output one of the box-drawing characters.

8.2 get, get0 and read

For input of single characters there are two predicates, **get(X)** and **get0(X)**. They both have one argument that becomes instantiated to the ASCII code representing a character read from the keyboard. The difference between them is that, in the case of **get(X)**, its argument will become instantiated only if the character read is "printable", i.e. not a function key, backspace, etc., while with **get0(X)** any character will do.

```
?- get(X).
```

will wait for the input of a single character. The character must be followed by a carriage return.

Here is a rule that reads a line of text typed at the keyboard and returns it as a list of words. It looks for the carriage return character (ASCII code 13) to recognize the end of the line and it recognizes the space (ASCII code 32) as a word separator.

```
read_word_list(L):-
    getchar(C), /* one character read ahead */
    read_word1(L, [], C). /* list is for building */
    /* of current word */
read_word1([], [], 13):-!.
read_word1([Word], Wlist, 13):-
    name(Word, Wlist),!.
read_word1(Words, Wlist, 32):-
    !,
    name(Word, Wlist),
    getchar(C),
    read_word1(L, [], C),
    append([Word], L, Words).
read_word1(Words, Wlist, C):-
    append(Wlist, [C], Wlist1),
    getchar(C1),
    read_word1(Words, Wlist1, C1).
getchar(C):-
    repeat,
        get0(C),
        acceptable_char(C),!.
acceptable_char(13). /* special case - <CR> */
acceptable_char(C):- /* only printable chars accepted */
    C >= 30,
    C =< 126.
```

This works by "carrying" a list of character codes that make up the current word being read in the second parameter of **read_word1** and converting this to an atom when a separator (space) or terminator (carriage return) is reached. The list of words making up the entire line is obtained using **append**.

This can easily be extended to fulfil more demanding roles. For example, the number of characters recognized as separators might be extended to include the comma, or upper case letters could automatically be converted to lower case.

For reading more than one character at a time there is the **read(X)** predicate.

?- read(X). will read an entire term, i.e. a constant, a variable or a structure, and will instantiate X to that term. When you input a term in response to the **read(X)** predicate you must terminate it with a full-stop and then press <Enter>. This is a very handy predicate for a quick solution to getting input from the user, but because of the need for the terminating full-stop it is usually not an acceptable approach for finished programs.

84

An approach that processes the input as in **read_word_list** given above is usually rather more acceptable.

8.3 Reading and writing sequential files

File handling is effected in a very simple manner by redirecting input and output. All the usual built-in predicates can be used as normal, except that they will either take their input from, or write their output to, a file.

To redirect the output to a file use the **tell(X)** predicate. It has one argument, which is the file name, which can be a variable, just as long as it dereferences to a valid file name at run time. The file is created if it does not exist. If it does exist it is overwritten, the previous contents being destroyed. The **told** predicate terminates output to the "tell" file, closes it, and causes output to be redirected to the screen. The following example directs user output to a file of the user's choice, then repeatedly reads a character from the user and writes it to that file, until \ is typed, when the file is closed.

```
copy_to_file:-
    write('Output file? '),
    read(File),
    tell(File),
    repeat,
        get0(C),
        put(C),
        (C = 92), /* ascii code for \ */
        !,
    told.
```

The predicates **see(F)** and **seen** are the input equivalents of **tell(X)** and **told**.

?- **see(datafile).** causes the input to be redirected to the file **datafile**. All predicates requiring input will get their input from this file until **seen** is executed.

There are also the predicates **seeing(X)** and **telling(X)**, both of which have a single parameter that will be matched with the current input and output files respectively. The built-in predicate **exists(X)** succeeds when the file X is instantiated to exists.

8.4 Logging a Prolog session

Often you would like to have a record of your Prolog session either to examine on screen or to print to file. Sometimes this is useful as proof that something worked, or as a reminder of a certain piece of interaction. But it is also very useful when you want to pore over an execution trace. With an execution trace it is often difficult to take in all the information that the trace offers while it is being produced. Also, it is not always possible to see far enough backwards through the trace to glean the necessary information that identifies the programming problem. The simplest way to get a permanent record of your interaction is to use the **log** built-in predicate. For example:

```
?- log(mylog).
```

will output a copy of all screen input and output to the file **mylog** until Prolog exits or **close_log** is called. For example:

```
?- close_log.
```

closes the file **mylog**. The file is always written to from the start, so if the file exists any previous contents will be lost.

Exercises 8

1. Modify **read_word_list** so that it automatically converts upper case to lower case.
2. Create a file that contains your name and address on several lines. Use **see(X)** to read from this file and use **read_word_list** to output your name and address as a series of lists to the screen. You will need to modify **read_word_list** so that it uses "line feed" (ASCII code 10) to detect the end of a line, rather than carriage return (ASCII code 13).
3. Put the atom **end_of_text** at the end of your address file. Define a rule that uses **read_word_list** to read from your address file and output each line as a list to the screen until the line consisting of **end_of_text** is reached. At this point it should invoke **seen** to terminate input from the file.

CHAPTER NINE
Searching

9.1 Networks and trees

Consider part of the Midlands rail network around Coventry:

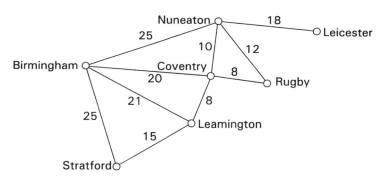

A basic problem of such networks is how to get from one place to another. What is needed is a search strategy. A search strategy may be optimal or non-optimal. An optimal solution minimizes the distance travelled; in a non-optimal one the distance travelled is ignored. For the moment we will consider only non-optimal solutions of getting from A to B.

First we need to represent the information given in the diagram in Prolog. We can use a series of unit ground clauses that record which places are connected and give the distance between them:

```
connected(birmingham, nuneaton, 25).
connected(nuneaton, leicester, 18).
connected(birmingham, coventry, 20).
connected(coventry, rugby, 8).
connected(coventry, leamington, 8).
```

```
connected(birmingham, leamington, 21).
connected(birmingham, stratford, 25).
connected(stratford, leamington, 15).
connected(nuneaton, rugby, 12).
connected(coventry, nuneaton, 10).
```

This describes all the connections in one direction only. We can extend this by adding a second predicate that allows a connection to be the other way too:

```
connected2(X, Y, D):-
    connected(X, Y, D).
connected2(X, Y, D):-
    connected(Y, X, D).
```

Using a different predicate name avoids the possibility of infinitely recursing.

We need to define a few frequently used terms before going any further. In a network, each connecting line is called an *arc*, at the end of each arc is a *node*, the starting point of our search is called the *starting node*, and the finishing point is called the *goal node* or the *terminal node*. The entire set of nodes is sometimes called the *search space*. A list of connected nodes (nodes that are joined by arcs) is called a *path* or sometimes a *search path*.

Once we have a starting node we can redraw our network as a tree using the starting node as the root. If we take Coventry as the starting node, then the tree is:

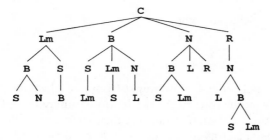

We draw this by starting at the root node and using the same arcs as the network but stopping whenever extending to a node would mean including that node on the path from the root twice. We refer to the nodes connected directly to a single node higher in the tree as *children* or *child nodes*. Hence Leamington, Birmingham, Nuneaton and Rugby are the child nodes of Coventry, which is the parent node of its children.

9.2 Finding successor nodes

In order to be able to do any sort of searching on a tree, we need a rule that finds all the directly connected nodes to a particular node that does not include any nodes that have already been visited. This means that the input must be the node to start from *and* the path of nodes already visited. We define a rule **next_node** that returns unvisited connected nodes:

```
next_node(Current, Next, Path):-
    connected2(Current, Next, _),
    not(member(Next, Path)).
```

This is sometimes called a *successor function* because it is capable of giving us all the successor nodes from any given node.

9.3 Depth-first search

In a depth-first search we search as deeply into the tree as possible at every node. That is whenever there is a choice of which node to visit next, we choose the one that is furthest from the root. It is equivalent to the preorder navigation of a tree that we met in Chapter 5. For example, a depth-first search starting at Coventry with the goal node set to Leicester visits the nodes Coventry, Leamington, Birmingham, Stratford, Nuneaton, Stratford, Birmingham, Birmingham, Stratford, Leamington, Leamington, Stratford, Nuneaton, Leicester.

The search must construct a list of nodes that represents the path from the start node to the goal node. This path is the result of the search; it shows us how to navigate through the nodes from the start node to the goal node. Note that it is not necessarily the same as all the nodes that are examined during the search. In general, far more nodes will be examined than will form part of the eventual search path. In the above example of a depth-first search from Coventry to Leicester we gave a list of all the nodes visited but the search path consists of the nodes Coventry, Birmingham, Nuneaton and Leicester.

```
The search can be expressed by the following algorithm:
goal_found = false
form a list containing the start node
if start_node = goal_node then
    goal_found = true
    exit
endif
for node = each successor node
    add node to list
    goal_found = depth_first(node,goal_node,list)
```

89

```
if goal_found then
    exit
endif
next node
```

Notice that this is a recursive algorithm. The notion of going deeply into the tree can easily be seen in the loop that contains the recursive call. This call is causing the search to deepen (move further away from the start node) before the loop takes the node across the tree (by returning into the loop), or in other words the loop is taking the search breadthwise through the tree and the recursive call is taking the search depthwise through the tree.

This can be translated very easily into Prolog. First, the boundary case is when the start node (first argument) is the same as the goal node (second argument). We need to supply the path taken so far as a third argument so that the rule for **next_node** can calculate the successor nodes. This third argument is not used by the boundary case as successor nodes are not required at the point that we reach the goal node. The fourth argument is for returning the path taken through the tree:

```
depth_first(Goal,Goal,_,[Goal]).
```

This means that when the start node is the same as the goal node, then the path consists of just that node. Now for the recursive part:

```
depth_first(Start, Goal, Visited, [Start|Path]):-
    next_node(Start, Next_node, Visited),
    depth_first(Next_node, Goal, [Next_node|Visited], Path).
```

This clause finds a successor node using **next_node** (notice that this is usually a choice point). The start node is made the head of the path. A recursive call carries the search on deeper from the successor node with the nodes visited now having the successor node at the head. We expect the recursive call to yield the path, which is the tail of the path we return.

Any failure of **depth_first** to find the goal node results in backtracking to the **next_node** rule, which selects a new successor node.

Consider the third and final arguments to **depth_first**. It might strike you as odd that we need two arguments to carry what is basically the same information, i.e. the path taken through the tree. The reason why we need two lists is plain to see when you consider what a query to find a particular path looks like. Say we want to do a depth-first search from Coventry to Leicester. Then the query is:

```
?- depth_first(coventry, leicester, [coventry], Path).
```

Notice that the argument for the visited nodes is the list containing just Coventry, indicating that at the time of calling this is the only visited node. The argument for the path is a variable. We start the search having visited one node and the recursive search instantiates path to the list of nodes that constitute the path to the goal node.

9.4 Breadth-first search

A breadth-first search is probably the easiest search to visualize. We start at the root node and examine all the immediately connected nodes in turn, i.e. each of the root node's children, stopping if we find the goal node. If we do not find the goal node we examine all the nodes connected to the nodes that we just examined (the grandchildren) and so on. It should not be hard to see why this is called breadth first: we are essentially moving across the tree breadthwise before moving down (further away from the root node).

For example, a breadth-first search starting with Coventry with the goal node of Leicester visits Leamington, Birmingham, Nuneaton, Rugby, then Birmingham, Stratford, Stratford, Leamington, Nuneaton, Birmingham, Leicester.

When the breadth-first search is expressed as an algorithm it seems a little different because we have to formalize how we build up a list of nodes to visit. The algorithm for breadth-first search is:

```
goal_found = false
form a list containing only the root node
loop until list is empty
    current_node = list head
    if current_node = goal node then
        goal_found = true
        exit loop
    else
        remove current_node from list
        add all the child nodes of current_node
        to end of the list
    endif
repeat
```

If we wish to retain the path that gets us to the goal node then this must be added to the algorithm. This increases the algorithm's complexity considerably because many paths are being considered at the same time. Consider the case where our start node is Coventry and the search path is initially just [coventry]. We now consider all the connected nodes to Coventry; this means that we are now considering each of the paths [leamington,coventry], [birmingham,coventry], [rugby,coventry] and [nuneaton,coventry]. We construct these path lists backwards as it is far more convenient for our program (we can find the first element of a list far easier than the last element). Only one of these paths will eventually prove fruitful and will interest us as the path to the goal node. What we have to do is keep a list of all the paths being considered and when the goal node is reached return the one that has been fruitful. At each recursive stage of the algorithm we extend a search path by each connected node.

How do we implement this algorithm in Prolog? We start with a convenient bit of packaging that takes the two input arguments, the start node and the goal node, and returns the path from one to the other. This calls **breadth_first1**.

The first argument to **breadth_first1** is the list of all active search paths, which starts off as having just one element, **[Start]**, which is the initial search path and contains only the start node. The second argument is the goal node, which is used to determine when the search has completed. The third argument is the path, which will become instantiated to the complete path from start node to goal node:

```
breadth_first(Start, Goal, Path):-
    breadth_first1([[Start]], Goal, Path).
```

The first clause for **breadth_first1** tests for the terminating condition, i.e. that the current node is the goal node, in which case it just succeeds, returning the path as being the nodes visited so far with the goal node inserted at the head.

```
breadth_first1([[Goal|Path]|_], Goal, [Goal|Path]).
```

The **next_node** predicate can then be used with the previously defined **findall** predicate to find the set of new paths. The first argument is a list of all the active search paths, each of which must be extended to all its connecting nodes. For example, the search path **[leamington,coventry]** must be extended to:

[birmingham,leamington,coventry] and

[stratford,leamington,coventry].

Given that a current path can be expressed as **[Current|Trail]**, the call to **findall** looks like this:

```
findall([Next,Current|Trail],
    next_node(Current, Next, Trail), NewPaths)
```

Note that **findall** generates a set of lists that is the set of new paths. This new set of paths can now be appended to the back of the set of path lists.

```
breadth_first1([[Current|Trail]|OtherPaths], Goal,
Path):-
    findall([Next,Current|Trail],
        next_node(Current,Next,Trail), NewPaths),
    append(OtherPaths, NewPaths, AllPaths),
    breadth_first1(AllPaths, Goal, Path).
```

This may not seem very easy to understand owing to the first argument being a list of lists and the subtle use of **findall**. One way to describe what is happening in this clause is by the following:

1. Remove first path from the current list of paths.
2. Find all the paths that can be extended from this.
3. Put these at the back of the list of paths.
4. Continue the search with the new list of paths.

This can now be used to find a non-optimal path between any two nodes. For example, to find a route from Coventry to Leicester we use the query:

```
?- breadth_first(coventry, leicester, Path).
```

This is how the set of paths grows for this query. We start with the only path being the list:

```
[coventry]
```

This path is extended by the following call to `findall`:

```
findall([Next,coventry], next_node(coventry,Next,[]),
NewPaths)
```

which instantiates new paths to:

```
[
    [leamington,coventry],
    [birmingham,coventry],
    [nuneaton,coventry],
    [rugby,coventry]
]
```

This is appended to the empty list, which of course yields the same list. Then we have the recursive call to `breadth_first1`. This takes the first list from the list of paths and makes this call to `findall`:

```
findall([Next,leamington,coventry],
    next_node(leamington,Next,[coventry]),
    NewPaths)
```

This instantiates `NewPaths` to:

```
[
    [birmingham,leamington,coventry],
    [stratford,leamington,coventry]
]
```

This is then appended to the tail of the input list which gives us the list:

```
[
    [birmingham,coventry],
    [nuneaton,coventry],
    [rugby,coventry],
    [birmingham,leamington,coventry],
    [stratford,leamington,coventry]
]
```

And the search continues until there is a match between the head of the first path list and the goal node.

9.5 Best-first search

The idea of the best-first search is to always extend the search from the most favourable node first. We saw with breadth-first search that an extended set of search paths was simply appended to the end of the current set. If we can discriminate in some way between these different search paths we can reorder them, which may speed up the searching. Defining what we mean by best can sometimes be a problem. In the case of the rail network we want the resulting path to have the shortest distance, so it makes sense to sort the paths based on their distance. To be able to do this we need a rule that can calculate the distance of a path. Consider:

```
path_distance([_], 0).
path_distance([A,B|Rest], D):-
    connected2(A, B, D1),
    path_distance([B|Rest], D2),
    D is D1 + D2.
```

This relies on each pair of nodes in the path being connected, which makes it a straightforward matter to sum the distances between each pair.

Our aim is to sort the paths by distance, so we need to be able to define "greater than" to use with our bubble sort rule. This will take two paths as arguments and succeed if the first path represents a greater distance:

```
gt(A, B):-
    path_distance(A, D1),
    path_distance(B, D2),
    D1 > D2.
```

To convert the breadth-first search to a best-first search only requires us to order the list of paths before making the recursive call to **breadth_first1**. Completing this is left as an exercise for the reader.

9.6 Distances

Other forms of distance measurements are often required when searching. The distance between two points in a search space can be defined in many ways. For example, take the distance between two points in a city such as Manhattan where you have to travel along either streets going north to south or east to west. If two different places are given co-ordinates X and Y, then the distance between them is the difference in the X values plus the distance in the Y values. This is sometimes called the Manhattan distance and it often occurs in searching problems.

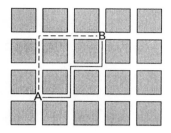

The two dimensional co-ordinates might be represented as `coord(X,Y)`. The distance between two such co-ordinates can be defined as:

```
dist(coord(X1,Y1), coord(X2,Y2)), D):-
    diff(X1, Y1, D1),
    diff(X2, Y2, D2),
    D is D1 + D2.
diff(A, B, D):-
    A >= B,
    D is A - B,
    !.
diff(A, B, D):-
    D is B - A.
```

We define `diff` to always give us a positive value; note the use of **cut** to prevent backtracking into the second clause for `diff` when we know it is not needed.

It is now very easy to define `gt(X,Y)` for our Manhattan distances as:

```
gt(X, Y):-
    X > Y.
```

Exercises

1. Draw a tree representing the Midlands Rail Network using Birmingham as the root node.
2. Give a list of all the nodes visited by a depth-first search from Birmingham to Rugby.
3. Give the path from Birmingham to Rugby obtained by the depth-first search in the previous question.
4. Implement the depth-first search in Prolog for question 2, but modify the second clause of **depth_first** to write the list of visited nodes to the screen.

5. Using the tree from question 1, give a list of all the nodes visited by a breadth-first search from Birmingham to Rugby.

6. Give the path from Birmingham to Rugby obtained by the breadth-first search in the previous question.

7. Implement the breadth-first search in Prolog for question 7, but modify the second clause of **breadth_first1** to show the list of new paths on the screen.

8. Convert the breadth-first search rule into a best-first rule by sorting the paths by their total distances.

CHAPTER TEN
Machine translation

10.1 Introduction

We perform translation of input strings in virtually every aspect of computer science. The best-known example of a non-trivial application is a compiler. This takes strings of source text and generates binary code corresponding to the intended meanings (as intended by the language designers, rather than the programmer!) of the source statements. The various forms that the statements of the source can take are usually rigidly defined by a "grammar".

The translation process is usually done in two phases:

1. *Syntactic analysis.* This is when the source code is checked for conformity to the defined syntax of the language, various structures are built, such as a parse tree, and symbol table entries made for ease of subsequent processing (this avoids the need to work with the original source).

2. *Semantic analysis.* This is when the code is generated corresponding to the original source. The meaning of the code is extracted and made apparent by the code generated.

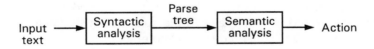

In the case of a natural language we can only successfully translate subsets of it as it is generally regarded as impossible to write down the syntax rules for an entire natural language. Apart from this limitation, the translation process is similar to that for a compiler: we perform syntactic analysis from which we build some internal representation of the input, then we take this and produce the necessary code (or actions) to execute what we understand the meaning of the input to be.

An excellent reference for parsing techniques using conventional programming languages is Rayward-Smith (1983). A Prolog perspective can be found in Warren & Periera (1981).

10.2 Backus Naur form

It is usual to express a grammar in Backus Naur form (BNF). For example:

```
<sentence> ::= <noun phrase> <verb phrase>
```

is the Backus Naur form for saying that a sentence can consist of a noun phrase followed by a verb phrase. It is called a production, as it shows us how a sentence is "produced" from less complicated components. Backus Naur form is particularly useful for describing what are called context-free grammars. These are grammars where these productions apply regardless of any other context.

The open and closed angled brackets indicate that the symbol inside the brackets is non-terminal, that is it is composed of other symbols. When a symbol is non-terminal it always appears on the left-hand side of some production of the grammar. A terminal symbol is something that cannot be broken down further. More realistically, there is no useful purpose in breaking it down further. For example an identifier in Pascal consists of characters, but for the purposes of parsing it is not very useful to consider the individual characters as the terminals. A scanner is often used to identify the terminal symbols of a language. These are mostly identifiers, labels, keywords, etc.

The Backus Naur production for a simple sentence can be directly expressed in Prolog by:

```
sentence(S):-
    append(NP, VP, S),
    noun_phrase(NP),
    verb_phrase(VP).
```

This can be made more efficient by eliminating the **append**. We can do this by introducing a second parameter to the goal, which stands for the remainder of the list when the predicate has completed:

```
sentence(S0, S):-
    noun_phrase(S0, S1),
    verb_phrase(S1, S).
```

So we would expect that when given the query:

```
?- sentence([the,boy,stood,on,the,burning,deck], []).
```

for the "noun phrase" goal:

```
S0 = [the,boy,stood,on,the,burning,deck]
    S1 = [stood,on,the,burning,deck]
```

i.e. the "noun phrase" goal takes the entire string,

`[the,boy,stood,on,the,burning,deck]`,

parses the first part, the boy, as the noun phrase and returns the remainder of the string as the list `[stood,on,the,burning,deck]`.

10.3 Complete example

The Backus Naur form for a tiny part of natural language is:

```
<noun phrase> ::= <determiner> <noun phrase 2>
<noun phrase> ::= <noun phrase 2>
<noun phrase 2> ::= <adjective> <noun phrase 2>
<noun phrase 2> ::= <noun>
<verb phrase> ::= <verb> <noun phrase>
<verb phrase> ::= <verb> <preposition phrase>
<verb phrase> ::= <verb>
<preposition phrase> ::= <preposition> <noun phrase>
<determiner> ::= the | a
<adjective> ::= burning | young ...
<noun> ::= boy | deck ...
<verb> ::= stood | ...
<preposition> ::= on | under | with | ...
```

We can apply a very straightforward and rather mechanical translation of this to Prolog:

```
sentence(S0, S):-
    noun_phrase(S0, S1),
    verb_phrase(S1, S).
noun_phrase(S0, S):-
    determiner(S0, S1),
    noun_phrase2(S1, S).
noun_phrase(S0, S):-
    noun_phrase2(S0, S).
noun_phrase2(S0, S):-
    adjective(S0, S1),
    noun_phrase2(S1, S).
noun_phrase2(S0, S):-
    noun(S0, S).
verb_phrase(S0, S):-
    verb(S0, S1),
```

```
        noun_phrase(S1, S).
    verb_phrase(S0, S):-
        verb(S0, S1),
        preposition_phrase(S1, S).
    verb_phrase(S0, S):-
        verb(S0, S).
    preposition_phrase(S0, S):-
        preposition(S0, S1),
        noun_phrase(S1, S).
    determiner([the|S], S).
    noun([boy|S], S).
    noun([deck|S], S).
    adjective([burning|S], S).
    verb([stood|S], S).
    preposition([on|S], S).
```

This only does the parsing, i.e. all it does is tell you that it can recognize
(parse) the input string. To be of any use at all we need it to build a parse
tree. This can be done quite simply by adding a third argument to all the
rules:

```
    sentence(S0, S, sentence(NP,VP)):-
        noun_phrase(S0, S1, NP),
        verb_phrase(S1, S, VP).
    noun_phrase(S0, S, np(D,NP2)):-
        determiner(S0, S1, D),
        noun_phrase2(S1, S, NP2).
    noun_phrase(S0, S, np(NP2)):-
        noun_phrase2(S0, S, NP2).
    noun_phrase2(S0, S, np2(A,NP2)):-
        adjective(S0, S1, A),
        noun_phrase2(S1, S, NP2).
    noun_phrase2(S0, S, np2(N)):-
        noun(S0, S, N).
    verb_phrase(S0, S, vp(V,NP)):-
        verb(S0, S1, V),
        noun_phrase(S1, S, NP).
    verb_phrase(S0, S, vp(V,P)):-
        verb(S0, S1, V),
        prepositional_phrase(S1, S, P).
    verb_phrase(S0, S, vp(V)):-
        verb(S0, S, V).
    prepositional_phrase(S0, S, prep(P,NP)):-
```

```
        preposition(S0, S1, P),
        noun_phrase(S1, S, NP).
    determiner([the|X], X, determiner(the)).
    noun([boy|X], X, noun(boy)).
    noun([deck|X], X, noun(deck)).
    adjective([burning|X], X, adjective(burning)).
    verb([stood|X], X, verb(stood)).
    preposition([on|X], X, preposition(on)).
```

The result of the query:

```
    ?- sentence([the,boy,stood,on,the,burning,deck], [], P).
```

is:

```
    P = sentence(np(determiner(the),np2(noun(boy))),
            vp(verb(stood),prep(preposition(on),np(determiner(the),
            np2(adjective(burning),np2(noun(deck))))))))
```

The structure that is returned will, in general, be used as input to the semantic analysis phase of our translation. The above structure is equivalent to the following tree.

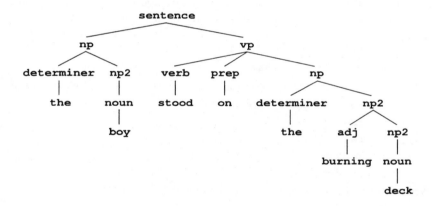

10.4 Example for data access

The following example is based on a language a little like SQL (structured query language), the standard language for accessing relational databases. A relational database conceptually comprises two-dimensional tables (relations), each of which has a number of named columns, and each data record forms a separate row (tuple) in a table. There is an example at the top of the next page. Here we have a table called Emp, containing employee information. It has three columns – Empno (employees' reference numbers), Empname (containing employees' names) and Job (containing their job titles) – and contains four data records (rows or tuples).

Emp		
Empno	Empname	Job
1	Smith	Clerk
2	Jones	Accountant
3	Peterd	Lawyer
4	King	Director

The Backus Naur form for part of the SQL grammar for accessing a database table is:

```
<query> ::= <select part>
<select part> ::= select [colname]⁺
<from part> ::= from <tablename>
```

The `[colname]`⁺ means that there is one or more occurrence of `colname`, i.e. the name of a column in the database table named `tablename`.

Using our example table "Emp", a query might be:

```
select empno empname from emp
```

which would display the reference number and name of all the employees in our Emp table. In order to parse this in Prolog, we assume that we have a rule, `read_word_list`, that takes the input string in its original form and converts it to a list of words. The code for such a rule was given in the previous chapter. An example of its use is:

```
?- read_word_list(Wlist).
```

which would wait for the user to enter a string. If the user enters the string:

```
select empno empname from emp;
```

then the response is:

```
Wlist = [select,empno,empname,from,emp]
```

Note that we are using the semicolon (ASCII code 59) as the terminating character in our input, rather than carriage return (ASCII code 13) used previously, and the code given for `read_word_list` should be modified accordingly.

The top-level goal `go` reads in the query, parses it and outputs the parse tree produced by the parsing process. It is defined by:

```
go:-
    read_word_list(Wlist),
    query(Wlist, [], Plist),
    write('Parse list is: '),
    write(Plist),nl.
```

The code to parse the query follows the Backus Naur definition in precisely the same way as our first example, with extra structures added for the return of a parse tree:

```
query(S0, S, q(Sel,F)):-
```

```
        select(S0, S1, Sel),
        from(S1, S, F).
    select([select|S0], S, select(Names)):-
        colnames(S0, S, Names).
    colnames(S0, S, [Name]):-
        colname(S0, S, Name).
    colnames(S0, S, [Name|Names]):-
        colname(S0, S1, Name),
        colnames(S1, S, Names).
    from([from|S0], S1, table(T)):-
        tablename(S0, S1, T).
```

Some example data to represent our Emp table is:

```
    colname([empno|S], S, empno).
    colname([empname|S], S, empname).
    colname([job|S], S, job).
    tablename([emp|S], S, emp).
```

10.5 Semantic analysis

Using the example query:

```
    select empname empno from emp;
```

produces the parse tree:

```
    q(select([empname,empno]), table(emp))
```

Notice that the column names have been collected in a list, as the number of them present in a query is not fixed.

The next problem is to take the parse tree as input and produce the answer to the query it represents. This is achieved most easily by writing rules that match with the various forms of the parse tree, and which then execute the necessary subgoals to achieve the corresponding effect. This is known as semantic analysis and is the process by which the meaning of the sentence is extracted and made to effect what it stands for.

For the above parse tree, it is necessary to define a rule that matches with this form of the parse tree:

```
    do_query(q(select(Colnames), table(Tname))):-
```

It would aid further processing if we translate column names into column numbers, so the first subgoal is:

```
    get_col_nums(Tname, Colnames, Colnums),
```

We then need to access the table with name **Tname** (assume the record is returned as a list):

```
    table(Tname, Rec),
```

We are then required to output the appropriate view of the record as determined by the specified columns in the "select" part of the parse tree:

```
output_view(Rec, 1, Columns),nl,
```

Finally, we are required to return all possible rows of the table, so the last subgoal is fail. We can add a second clause for **do_query** to terminate neatly the solution to the query:

```
do_query(_):-
    write('Query answered'),nl.
```

The code for the various subgoals is very straightforward, and for the sake of completeness is given here.

```
output_view(_, _, []):-!.
output_view([Hcol|Rest], Fieldno, [Fieldno|Restnums]) :-
    !,
    write(Hcol),write(' '),
    Next_field is Fieldno + 1,
    output_view(Rest, Next_field, Restnums).
output_view([_|Rest], Fieldno, Nums):-
    Next_field is Fieldno + 1,
    output_view(Rest, Next_field, Nums).
get_col_nums(_, [], []):-!.
get_col_nums(Tname, [Col|Colrest], [Num|Numrest]):-
    col_number(Tname, Col, Num),
    get_col_nums(Tname, Colrest, Numrest).
col_number(emp, empno, 1).
col_number(emp, empname, 2).
col_number(emp, job, 3).
```

This is some example data for the Emp table:

```
table(emp,[1,smith,clerk]).
table(emp,[2,jones,accountant]).
table(emp,[3,peters,lawyer]).
table(emp,[4,king,director]).
```

Exercises 10

1. Extend the grammar in Backus Naur form to include the SQL **where** clause for a single condition. For example, a query might now be:

    ```
    select empno empname from emp where job equals lawyer;
    ```

2. Modify the Prolog for the parser to allow parsing of the new grammar suggested in question 1.

3. Modify the Prolog for the semantic analyser to cope with the amendment of question 1.

CHAPTER ELEVEN
Large programs

11.1 Introduction

Software engineering is concerned with sound design and implementation, efficient use of resources and maintainability. These rapidly become important considerations as code size increases. As with any computer language all of these issues are of concern to the Prolog developer and, perhaps fortunately, many of the lessons learnt using conventional languages can be usefully employed when coding in Prolog.

11.2 The top level

What do large Prolog programs look like at the topmost level? Or, to put this another way, how do we effect control over our large Prolog programs? The answer is in much the same way as with a conventional program. Typically we can expect a conventional program to have the following structure:

```
begin
    initialise
    loop
        read command
        obey command
    until exit condition
end
```

The bold words are the sort of instructions that are available in conventional languages. This is typical of an interactive program. In many cases we might expect a main menu to be sandwiched between the "loop" and "until". The bold words are not available in Prolog, but we can easily achieve the same effect. Consider:

```
rap:-
    initialise,
    repeat
        top_menu(X),
    fail.
```

This is the main driving "loop" of a 3000-line program. I always indent between a **repeat** and a **fail** to make the construct stand out. **initialise** is a rule that sets up some session specific information.

We can use a menu construct (which in some Prologs is supplied as a built-in predicate, but can easily be defined in any Prolog) to allow the program to invoke any of a set of subgoals. The **fail** ensures that we always return to the master menu (whether the subgoals succeed or fail).

This is how the menu facility is defined:

```
top_menu:-
    display_top_menu,
    read_line(X),
    execute(X).
```

The rule **read_line(X)** is a general-purpose utility that reads user input and converts it to an atom. It is defined thus:

```
read_line(A):-
    get0(C),
    process_char(C, L),
    name(A, L).
process_char(13, []):-!.
process_char(C, [C|Rest]):-
    get0(C1),
    process_char(C1, Rest).
```

The menu is displayed by the following code:

```
display_top_menu:-
    write('> Menu select:'),nl,
    write('(1) Start new rule-base'),nl,
    write('(2) Test or edit existing rule-base'),nl,
    write('(3) Explain on'),nl,
    write('(4) Explain off'),nl,
    write('(5) Restart'),nl,
    write('(6) Exit'),nl.
```

This consists of nothing more than a set of **write** statements. The appropriate goal is then executed by one of the following clauses:

```
execute(1):-
```

```
    init_rule_base.
execute(2):-
    test_or_edit.
execute(3):-
    assertz(tron).
execute(4):-
    retract(tron).
execute(5):-
    resolve_all.
execute(6):-
    halt.
```

Execution of the **display_top_menu** goal will cause the following to be displayed:

```
(1) Start new rule-base
(2) Test or edit existing rule-base
(3) Explain on
(4) Explain off
(5) Restart
(6) Exit
```

Note that the potentially infinite backtracking is terminated here just by calling **halt**. It is also possible to terminate such a loop by using **cut** to remove the choice point created by **repeat**.

Selection of "1" will cause **execute**'s parameter to be instantiated to 1, which causes the rule **init_rule_base** to be executed.

Another easy to implement facility is to allow the user a choice of actions from the input of a single character. This has the same form as using the menu but without the need for any display:

```
choose:-
    read_line(X),
    execute(X).
```

The **execute** part can then selected by the appropriate letter.

```
execute(i):-
    init_rule_base.
execute(t):-
    test_or_edit.
execute(e):-
    explain('explain').
execute(n):-
    noexplain.
```

This method can be combined with the menus to give the user choice of directly entering commands by a single letter or selecting from a menu.

The addition of the rule:

```
execute(m):-
    top_menu.
```

does this. The user can enter commands in a direct fashion when the commands are known. Alternatively, by typing **m**, the user can opt to select from a menu.

11.3 Top-down design for Prolog programs

Large Prolog programs can conveniently be defined using conventional methodologies if they embrace the concepts of modularity. In particular, the much used "top-down" design method is appropriate. In case the terms "top-level procedure" and "bottom-level procedure" are unfamiliar to the reader, here are their definitions:

- top-level procedure: the main (driving) procedure;
- bottom-level procedure: a procedure that does not call other procedures.

The top-down design method can then be stated, in a form amended for the Prolog language, as:

1. Start at the top level.
2. Sketch out a goal sequence for this level in English.
3. Specify structures required at this level.
4. Progressively formalize into Prolog code identifying the function and parameters of each subgoal.
5. Complete specification rigorously; check the declarative semantics of all variables and structures.
6. Go to the next level down, that is take each subgoal in turn, and apply step 2 to it. This may, and usually does, involve defining yet more subgoals.

The method is applied until all levels are specified rigorously.

The reason why this is a good method is that it allows us to think about a small but logically consistent subset of code at a time. When the code for a rule is designed and a subgoal is defined we do not need to worry about how the subgoal is going to achieve its function, we just assume that we will be able to design the subgoal when we get to it and if necessary we will define more subgoals to be called by this subgoal in order to make the problem tractable. We can expect always to be able to design rules effectively in this way as long as the preceding design and formulation of data structures has been sound. Sometimes the solution may not be the most effective in terms of performance or memory use, but these problems can be examined separately. We should endeavour to keep rules short in order to make their function and operation as clear as possible and their validation as easy as possible. A large part of this involves giving variables and rules meaningful names. Another important factor in making subgoals easily read and easily verified is the use of neat formatting. Putting a comment immediately before each rule that identifies the input and output parameters and their relationship is to be recommended.

Conventionally, it is always hoped that a procedure can be verified visually by determining that the correct relationship holds between the input and output parameters. This is often quite difficult because of the procedural nature of the code, which makes it hard to visualize the effect of the running code from its static code statements. With Prolog we find ourselves in a far better position because Prolog is declarative, and it should always be possible to see the run time implications directly from a visual inspection of the code. However, if we use asserts and retracts frequently we soon find ourselves with the same problems as our less fortunate conventional coders. The declarative nature of Prolog is weakened with every assert and retract used and so these predicates must be avoided wherever possible. Alternatively, their use should be localized to as few rules as possible so that the majority of the code is isolated from their effect.

11.4 Encapsulation and abstract data types (ADTs)

The idea of an abstract data type is a very simple one. We specify procedures that perform the operations that we require regardless of how any particular data structure might be used to effect these operations. Then, quite independently, we implement these procedures to do the necessary operations to the chosen data structures. Only these procedures have access to the data structures, and the data structures can only be altered by use of these procedures. This effectively divides the code into those calls that have some specific purpose, but no knowledge of how this purpose is achieved, and the procedures that implement these purposes and operate on the data structures internally. This sounds similar to the top-down design approach, but it has the important additional point that the data structures are entirely hidden from view, they are encapsulated within the abstract data type and only those procedures that form part of the type have knowledge of and access to the actual data structures.

In practice, it can be difficult to prevent access to a particular data structure, but we keep to the spirit of the idea by simply passing arguments as variables that represent the structure to the procedures that constitute the ADT and receiving them back while only ever allowing the procedures of the ADT to actually look at them. We often call these arguments handles to the data structure.

A typical example would be the creation and manipulation of an ordered list. Our ADT would consist of predicates for creating, adding an element, deleting an element and accessing an element. Their external appearance might be:

```
create_ordered_list(-L)          return a new handle
add_to_ordered_list(+L,          add an element to the list given by the
   +Element)                        handle L
delete_from_ordered_list         delete an element from the list given
   (*L, + Element)                  by the handle L
access_ordered_list(+L, +N,      access the Nth element of list given by
   -Element)                        the handle L
```

Here I have used + to denote an input argument, - to denote an output argument, and * to denote input and output.

In implementing this in Prolog we have the choice of making L itself the data structure (as long as the user treats it as a handle all will be well) or using it as an identifier for the actual data structure, which is more secure, but a little harder to code and will necessitate the use of **assert** in order to store the data structures used between accesses (these can be retrieved from the database using the handle).

An important advantage of using an ADT is that we can entirely recode one to use completely different representations and algorithms without having to alter any code that uses the ADT. Efficiency and resource concerns can be entirely encapsulated by the ADT effectively isolating the rest of the code from these concerns.

11.5 Memory management

In most conventional languages memory must be allocated to data structures before they can be used, and deallocated when they are discarded. This is a fairly complex business that often causes severe problems. It is not uncommon for even commercial packages to have problems in this area, sometimes called memory leakage, when unused memory is not properly deallocated. This eventually causes failure as a result of the system running out of memory. Other typical problems involve overwriting of one structure with another or freeing memory areas that are still required. Luckily, for the Prolog programmer, these problems do not exist. Memory is allocated for your structures quite automatically and a garbage collector is used to reclaim memory areas that are no longer used. However, garbage collection is a costly operation and the comments made in Chapter 7 should be heeded. In particular, it should be noted that failure-driven loops require no garbage collection, whereas recursive calls may cause problems unnecessarily if they can easily be replaced by an equivalent failure-driven form.

11.6 Failure-driven and recursive loops

Constructs in which a loop is effectively established by using **fail** to iterate over a set of solutions or which use **repeat** and **fail** to create an infinite loop are called "failure-driven loops", for the obvious reason that it is
the failure that is forcing the iteration. This is not the only way we can program to get the looping effect. Our example above could be written:

```
rap:-
    initialise,
    rap2.
rap2:-
    top_menu(X),
    rap2.
```

Notice that here **top_menu(X)** would always need to succeed for the
looping (or recursion) to continue. To a logician, and for many Prolog programmers, the second solution is more elegant. Unfortunately, many
Prolog implementations, including this one, make harder work of it, using
more and more stack space as the recursion deepens. This may cause garbage collections (reclamation of memory space) to occur at unpredictable
times, which can make the performance of the program unacceptable. In
the failure-driven loop, each failure allows the Prolog system to reclaim all
the space used directly.

My own view is that, in general, a failure-driven loop is acceptable for
simple iterative operations but should be avoided when being used to manipulate complex, and what are usually recursive, data structures.

Exercises

1. Write a menu-driven program that allows the user to assert, retract
   and list facts to the screen. Each of these should be menu options.
   Read facts from the user using the **read(X)** predicate as described in
   Chapter 8.
2. Use top-down design to implement a storage and retrieval system for
   names, telephone numbers and addresses. Your system should allow
   the user facilities for searching on partial matches with the data. The
   user should also be able to browse and have some editing facilities,
   for example it should be possible to alter part of an address.
3. Give Prolog code for the ADT described in this chapter. Do not pass
   the actual data structure, but only a handle. The actual data structure
   can be stored using **assert** in the form:

   ```
   ordered_list(handle, data_structure)
   ```

   where handle is a unique identifier, i.e. 1 for the first used, 2 for the
   second and so on.

Prolog and expert systems

12.1 Expert systems

An expert system encodes and utilizes expertise in some domain that is often learnt or elicited from a human. We expect it to show reasonably intelligent behaviour within the domain being considered. Typical examples of early successful expert systems are: DENDRAL (Lindsay et al. 1980), a system for identifying chemical compounds; MYCIN (Feigenbaum 1979, Buchanan & Shortliffe 1984), a system for diagnosing bacterial infections; and PROSPECTOR (Duda et al. 1979), a system for identifying mineral deposits.

We expect an expert system to be capable of encoding knowledge about some domain in a particularly straightforward manner, i.e. the knowledge must be encoded quite directly and not need reducing into algorithms. We also expect an expert system to be capable of explaining its line of reasoning and be able to justify the results it produces.

12.2 Suitability of Prolog

Prolog is a suitable language for the development of expert system-type programs for several reasons. These are discussed in the following sections.

12.2.1 Rule based

Any program written in Prolog is a series of rules. The rule-based approach has advantages over the conventional approach to writing programs:
- Rules can work largely independently of each other (the whole system does not collapse if one is removed in the same way that a

FORTRAN or Pascal program might if one line were to be removed). The system will produce some sort of sense even when incorrect (with conventional programs the outcome is very unpredictable and will often lead to a program crash).

- A set of rules is a natural structure for expertise. Many human skills, perhaps most, are accomplished by learning rules.
- Rules can be incrementally updated. The example concerning insurance in Chapter 2 could have more rules and have the head **risk_for_capacity** appended to the rule base without affecting the validity of those already there.

12.2.2 Declarative

To a large extent, Prolog is declarative, which can make program design very like program specification. This makes rules concise and amenable to verification by inspection. Any assignment of variables is effected by unification. There are no explicit decisions or branches. There is virtually no execution logic to specify. This style of specification is ideal for the development of a rule base for an expert system that allows real-world rules to translate in a fairly direct way to program rules.

12.2.3 Explanations

A Prolog program can be made to explain its own reasoning in a very straightforward manner and an example is given later in the chapter.

12.2.4 Backward and forward chaining

The basic theorem-proving aspect of Prolog is backward chaining: this means that the Prolog system starts with what has to be proved and attempts to build a proof tree for it. But, as Prolog is a complete programming language, there is nothing to prevent us coding our own inference engine in Prolog which forward chains. An inference engine is simply a program that can manipulate a known set of facts and rules to produce (infer) new facts. In forward chaining we do not try to prove any particular goal, but deduce whatever we can from the known rules and facts. In practice, Prolog turns out to be a highly suitable language for writing inference engines. A Prolog program that does this is discussed later in this chapter.

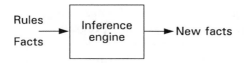

12.2.5 Top-down design

Prolog naturally encourages top-down design when writing programs. Horn clauses naturally break down problems into an hierarchy of subgoals with local parameters. Hence, the natural design method is to start with the principal goal, break it down into subgoals while identifying the variables needed at this level, and then repeat the process for each subgoal. This is exactly the top-down design method of conventional software engineering. Thus, Prolog comes with a sound design methodology that facilitates the construction of expert system rule bases.

12.2.6 First-order logic

The value of Prolog being based on first-order logic is that this is a mathematically sound vehicle for reasoning and modelling our problem areas. It helps us in formulating logically consistent rules, forcing us to think clearly by directly expressing our programs as logic. An example of where this can be seen to work is in the following problem.

Consider the following statements:

Pam knows Mike's telephone number.
Mary has the same telephone number as Mike.
Pam dials Mike's telephone number.

Can we deduce that Pam knows Mary's telephone number?

Common sense tells us that we cannot, but there definitely is a sense in which Pam knows Mary's telephone number – she knows the number but not the fact that it is Mary's. To put it another way, Pam knows Mary's number but only as Mike's number. The matter is easily resolved when we express the facts in Prolog, because we are forced to state what we mean by "knows". If we want "knows" to express the relation between a person and another person and their telephone number, then this suggests that the second person in the relation and their number should be a structure. This clearly allows us to express that it is the link between a person and their telephone number that is important, not just the number. So we can express the example as follows.

```
knows(pam, mikestel(57733)).
marystel(57733).
dials(pam, 57733).
```

and make the queries:

```
?- dials(pam, X),marystel(X).
X = 57733
yes
?- knows(pam, marystel(X)).
no
```

This is clear, concise and unambiguous. It involves no procedural information, just the declaration of the required relation. Of course, it is still possible for the muddle-headed programmer to define nonsense in Prolog, but it is much easier for the clear-minded to express their ideas simply and directly.

In conclusion, Prolog offers enormous advantages to the expert system builder.

12.3 An expert system in Prolog

We are going to construct an expert system to give careers advice to students. It is going to be very simple and the actual knowledge it encodes should not be taken very seriously! The system will interact with the user, asking questions to establish information that is needed to execute the rules. It will attempt to identify a profession by establishing that its requirements are met and that the student's motivations are compatible.

For the purposes of this example we will just take a few professions and list their requirements and what the jobs offer:

Firefighter. Requires: bravery, very good health, no fear of heights. Offers: excitement.

Solicitor. Requires: good academic grades, good memory, methodical thinking. Offers: good pay.

Police officer. Requires: bravery, fair or good academic grades, very good health. Offers: excitement.

These can be simply encoded in Prolog as subgoals listing these attributes:

```
recommended_profession(firefighter):-
    brave(very),
    health(very_good),
    fear_of_heights(none),
    likes_excitement(greatly).
recommended_profession(solicitor):-
    academic_grades(good),
    memory(good),
    thinking(methodical),
    likes_good_pay(greatly).
recommended_profession(police_officer):-
    brave(very),
    (academic_grades(fair);academic_grades(good)),
    health(very_good),
    likes_excitement(greatly).
```

We require our expert system to start with the first profession and try to establish whether it is suitable for the person being "interviewed". To do this it must ask the person for any information it does not know, and keep track of this information in case it is needed for another rule.

A useful utility would be a predicate that displayed a menu of choices with a prompt, and returned the value that had been selected by the user. We will make the assumption that each choice on the menu starts with a different letter, so the user will make a selection by pressing a single key that indicates the first letter of the chosen profession. The selections will be given as a list of atoms. We will define the **menu** predicate immediately:

```
menu(Prompt, Selections, Choice):-
    nl,
    write(Prompt),nl,nl,
    display_selections(Selections),
    nl,
    write('Type 1st letter <Enter> '),
    get(C),nl,
    get_choice(C,Selections,Choice),
    nl.
display_selections([]):-
    nl.
display_selections([H|T]):-
    tab(5),
    write(H),nl,
    display_selections(T).
get_choice(C, [], Choice):-
    write('Illegal selection'),nl,!.
get_choice(C, [Choice|T], Choice):-
    name(Choice, [C|_]),!.
get_choice(C, [_|T], Choice):-
    get_choice(C, T, Choice).
```

The rule **get_choice** illustrates a very neat way of using **name** and parameter matching to effect the required result. We can then define a rule for finding out how brave someone is as:

```
brave(X):-
    askable(brave),
    menu('How brave are you?', [very, average,
    fair, poor],Y),
    assertz(brave(Y)),
    retract(askable(brave)),
    X = Y,!.
```

We use **askable** to keep track of the questions that can be asked, and we retract **askable(brave)** when the question is answered. Also notice that we delay trying to unify "X" with the result from **menu** until after the **assertz** and **retract**. This is because when we use the rule **brave** we will be trying to establish a goal such **as brave(very)**, so if the user admitted to being only averagely brave then the **menu** predicate would fail and we would not get the answer asserted into the database. We assert it so that we will not need to ask for it again.

We can produce rules for the other attributes in a similar fashion:

```
health(X):-
    askable(health),
    menu('How good is your health?',
    [very_good,average,fair,poor],Y),
    assertz(health(Y)),
    retract(askable(health)),
    X = Y,!.
fear_of_heights(X):-
    askable(fear_of_heights),
    menu('What is your fear of heights?',
    [none,slight,moderate,extreme],Y),
    assertz(fear_of_heights(Y)),
    retract(askable(fear_of_heights)),
    X = Y,!.
likes_excitement(X):-
    askable(likes_excitement),
    menu('Do you like excitement?',
    [greatly,moderately,slightly,no],Y),
    assertz(likes_excitement(Y)),
    retract(askable(likes_excitement)),
    X = Y,!.
academic_grades(X):-
    askable(academic_grades),
    menu('Are your academic grades?',
    [good,fair,poor],Y),
    assertz(academic_grades(Y)),
    retract(askable(academic_grades)),
    X = Y,!.
memory(X):-
    askable(memory),
    menu('Is your memory?',
    [good,fair,poor],Y),
```

```
        assertz(memory(Y)),
        retract(askable(memory)),
        X = Y, !.
thinking(X):-
        askable(thinking),
        menu('Is your thinking?',
        [methodical,vague],Y),
        assertz(thinking(Y)),
        retract(askable(thinking)),
        X = Y, !.
likes_good_pay(X):-
        askable(likes_good_pay),
        menu('Do you like good pay?',
        [greatly,moderately,slightly,no],Y),
        assertz(likes_good_pay(Y)),
        retract(askable(likes_good_pay)),
        X = Y, !.
```

Finally we need to have a set of facts for the "askable" questions.

```
askable(brave).
askable(health).
askable(fear_of_heights).
askable(likes_excitement).
askable(academic_grades).
askable(memory).
askable(thinking).
askable(likes_good_pay).
```

In this form we can run our expert system by typing the query:

```
?- recommended_profession(X).
```

12.4 Explanation

A proper expert system really needs an explanation facility, so that when the expert system has reached a conclusion we can ask it why it has reached that conclusion and get some meaningful response.

There are many ways of achieving this, depending on the details of the system. We can achieve an explanation very easily by just writing one in English in the head of each recommended_profession clause. For example:

```
recommended_profession(firefighter, ['very brave',
    'very good health','no fear of heights',
    'likes excitement']):-
```

```
brave(very),
health(very_good),
fear_of_heights(none),
likes_excitement(greatly).
```

The second parameter can then be used, when the rule succeeds, to indicate the subgoals that were satisfied, thereby explaining why "firefighter" was chosen.

This gives an adequate trace for a small example like this, but is not adequate in the general case, especially when our rules are deeply nested.

A more general solution is to add a second parameter to each goal head, which explains why that particular goal succeeds, using information passed back from the second parameter of the subgoal. We can include additional information as to whether the user simply stated that something was true or whether the expert system deduced it from subgoals. For example:

```
recommended_profession(firefighter,
    recommended_profession(deduced([B,H,F,L]))):-
    brave(very, B),
    health(very_good, H),
    fear_of_heights(none, F),
    likes_excitement(greatly, L).
brave(X, stated('How brave are you',X)):-
    askable(brave),
    menu('How brave are you?',
    [very,averagely,fair,poor],Y),
    assertz(brave(Y,stated('How brave are you',
    Y))),
    retract(askable(brave)),
    X = Y, !.
```

We add second parameters in the same way to all our goals that are not simply for utility purposes (such as **get_choice**).

The explanation we now get looks quite complicated. For example:

```
recommended_profession(deduced(
    [stated('How brave are you', very),
    stated(health,very_good),
    stated(fear_of_heights,none),
    stated(likes_excitement,greatly)])).
```

This might not be very readable, but it is an easy matter to define an "explanation sub-system" to make sense of it. This will consist of a rule that takes the recommended profession and the above structure as input, and writes out an English explanation that corresponds to the input structure.

```
explanation_subsystem(R, recommended_profession(X)):-
```

```
      write('The profession '),
      write(R),
      write(' was chosen because:'),nl,nl,
      explain(X).
explain(stated(X,Y)):-
      write('To the question: '),
      write(X),
      write('? You answered: '),
      write(Y).
explain(deduced(L)):-
      write('It was deduced because: '),nl,
      explain(L).
explain([]).
explain([H|T]):-
      explain(H),
      explain(T).
```

This gives a readily understood trace.

12.5 Inference engines

We can write more advanced expert systems by writing our own inference engines. We can make these backward chain, like the example above, forward chain or deal with certainty factors; in fact we can tailor them to do precisely what we want them to do.

In order to give a more natural syntax to our rules we can define a number of operators as prefix and infix. This avoids the use of lots of brackets. This is really a cosmetic issue, but it removes much of the Prolog flavour and makes our rules easier to write and understand. This is how we define them using the op/3 built-in predicate:

```
:- op(1100, fx, forward_rule).
:- op(1100, fx, backward_rule).
:- op(1100, fx, deduce).
:- op(1080, fx, if).
:- op(1070, xfx, then).
:- op(1060, xfy, and).
:- op(1050, xfx, can).
:- op(1050, xfx, has).
:- op(1050, xfx, has_property).
:- op(1050, xfx, found_in).
:- op(1030, xfx, isa).
:- op(1030, xfx, with_certainty).
```

We use **forward_rule** and **backward_rule** for declaring the rules, and these are defined as prefix, that is they come before a single argument that will be the rule. We use **deduce** to invoke backward chaining: it prefixes a single argument that is the goal to be proved. The **if** is for constructing rules and it is also prefix, coming before the premises and the conclusion. The premises and the conclusion are connected by the infix operator **then**, which comes between them. Where there is more than one premise they are joined by the infix operator **and**. Then there are various descriptors, for example: fish can swim, tiger is a cat, etc. Finally, there is the infix operator **with_certainty**, which will be used for attaching certainty values to rules.

Here are some example rules and facts:

```
forward_rule if
        X isa fish
    and
        X found_in ocean
    then
        X has_property edible.
forward_rule if
        X can swim
    and
        X has gills
    then
        X isa fish.

fact(cod can swim).
fact(cod has gills).
fact(cod found_in ocean).
```

12.5.1 Forward chaining

This works by repeatedly executing the rules and asserting whatever can be deduced from them. The new facts that have been deduced are added into the set of known facts and then the process is repeated. When nothing more can be deduced the system stops.

The basic idea is to take every rule of the "if condition(s) then conclusion" form and each time the condition(s) can be satisfied the conclusion is asserted. This is known as a cycle of the forward chainer. It cycles through the rules for as long as new assertions are being made. This is an unguided strategy as no particular goal is being targeted, rather anything that can be derived from the rules is derived. Here we initialize the forward chaining and call the main forward chainer:

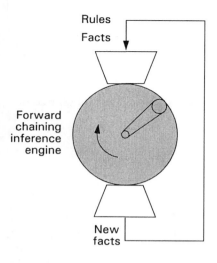

Rules
Facts

Forward
chaining
inference
engine

New
facts

```
fc:-
    initialise,
    forward_chain,
    write('Forward chaining finished.'),nl.
initialise:-
    abolish(proof_cycle),
    abolish(new_assert),
    assert(proof_cycle(0)).
```

Now we have the main cycling part of the forward chainer. This uses a **repeat/fail** loop to iterate over the deduction process. It exits from the potentially infinite loop by checking whether new assertions have been made. If they have not then **cut** is called to remove the backtrack point created by the repeat. At each iteration it tries to prove all the rules in the database.

```
forward_chain:-
    repeat,
    (
    (new_assertions(X),X=0,!)
    ;
    update_proof_cycle,
    proof_cycle(N),
    explain(['Proof cycle ',N]),
    (forward_rule Rule),
    forward_prove(Rule),
    fail
    ).
```

```
update_proof_cycle:-
    retract(proof_cycle(N)),
    M is N + 1,
    assert(proof_cycle(M)).
new_assertions(1):-
    proof_cycle(0),!. /* first cycle so no new assertions
needed */
new_assertions(1):-
    new_assert,
    !,
    abolish(new_assert).
new_assertions(0).
```

Now for the part that actually does the inferencing. The first clause is trivial as it just tests whether the right-hand side has already been proved and, if it has, it does nothing. The second clause attempts to satisfy the left-hand side of the rule; if it can, it asserts the right-hand side as a fact. Note that it is simply trying to satisfy the left-hand side as a series of facts; there is no hidden backward chaining going on! The third clause deals with a conjunction in the left-hand side of a rule.

```
forward_prove(if LHS then RHS):-
    proved(RHS),!.
forward_prove(if LHS then RHS):- /* match on a rule, then
fc on LHS */
    !,
    forward_prove(LHS),
    explain([LHS,' has been proved']),
    my_assert(fact(RHS)),/*see code on disk */
    explain(['Asserting ',RHS]).
forward_prove(A and B):-
    !,
    forward_prove(A),
    forward_prove(B).
forward_prove(A):-
    fact(A).
proved(X):-
    fact(X).
```

12.5.2 Backward chaining

For completeness, we will define an inference engine for backward chaining. A backward chainer must start with a user-supplied goal that it is required to prove. It matches the goal with the right-hand side of a rule,

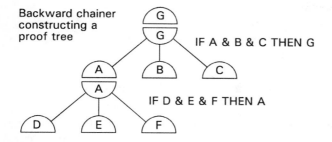

Backward chainer constructing a proof tree

IF A & B & C THEN G

IF D & E & F THEN A

then attempts to satisfy the left-hand side of the rule. If it fails it looks for a new match for the goal until there are no more. As with forward chaining, this uses "if condition(s) then conclusion" type rules, commonly called productions. This is a more focused approach than forward chaining. A particular goal is being aimed at and the system tries to construct a proof for the goal in question.

Here are the same example rules declared as backward:

```
backward_rule if
      X isa fish
and
      X found_in ocean
then
      X has_property edible.
backward_rule if
      X can swim
and
      X has gills
then
      X isa fish.
```

We use these with the same facts as for the forward chaining example.

The backward chainer is a very straightforward piece of Prolog. The first rule is just convenient packaging:

```
deduce RHS :-
backward_prove(RHS).
```

The first clause of **backward_prove** is satisfied if the right-hand side is a fact. The second clause attempts to find a rule where there is a match on the right-hand side of the rule with the goal currently being proved. If it can find such a rule it backward chains on the left-hand side. The third clause deals with a conjunction occurring in the left-hand side of a rule:

```
backward_prove(RHS):-
    fact(RHS),
    explain([RHS,' is a known fact.']).
```

```
backward_prove(RHS):-
    (backward_rule if LHS then RHS),
    explain([RHS,' matches rule with LHS ',LHS]),
    backward_prove(LHS).
backward_prove(A and B):-
    backward_prove(A),
    backward_prove(B).
```

It is a simple matter to augment the inference engine with the ability to ask the user questions. We need to assert into the database what goals can be regarded as askable. For example, we might assert:

```
askable(X can fly).
```

If a goal is askable and cannot be satisfied by any of the rules defined so far, then we construct a question to ask the user employing a simple translation table. We present the question to the user and act according to the reply:

```
backward_prove(A):-
    askable(A),
    ask(A).
ask(A):-
    translations(A,Q),
    writelist(Q),
    write('? (y/n) '),
    getyn(Ans),
    retract(askable(A)),
    Ans = 121, /* 'y' */
    assert(fact(A)).
translations(X isa Y, ['Is ',X,' a ',Y]).
translations(X has Y, ['Does ',X,' have ',Y]).
translations(X has_property Y, ['Does ',X,' have property
',Y]).
translations(X can Y, ['Can ',X,' ',Y]).
translations(X found_in Y, ['Is ',X,' found in ',Y]).
```

12.5.3 Backward chaining with certainty factors

Certainty factors are associated with each rule and fact. They describe how much faith is to be placed in the relevant rule or fact. The certainties are combined in the conditional part of the rule by taking the minimum value of the conditional goals and multiplying this by the certainty value of the rule. As with the two methods above, production rules are used but with an extra **with_certainty** C part. A threshold can be imposed on the certainty value in order to abandon unprofitable searches. See clause 2 of

backward_prove_with_certainty. For example, here are some facts about flu with their certainty factors:

```
fact(george has aching_limbs with_certainty 0.9).
fact(george has_property sweaty with_certainty 0.7).
fact(george has fever with_certainty 0.6).
```

And some rules we can use with these:

```
backward_rule if
    X has temperature with_certainty C1
    and
    X has aching_limbs with_certainty C2
    then
    X has flu with_certainty 0.9.
backward_rule if
    X has_property sweaty with_certainty C1
    and
    X has fever with_certainty C2
    then
    X has temperature with_certainty 0.9.
```

The Prolog code for backward chaining with certainties is a modified form of the backward chainer given above.

```
deduce RHS with_certainty C :-
    backward_with_certainty(RHS with_certainty C, C).
backward_with_certainty(RHS with_certainty C, C):-
    fact(RHS with_certainty C).
backward_with_certainty(RHS with_certainty C, C):-
    (backward_rule if LHS then RHS with_certainty C1),
    backward_with_certainty(LHS, C2),
    C is C1*C2,
    C > 0.
backward_with_certainty(A and B, C):-
    backward_with_certainty(A, C1),
    backward_with_certainty(B, C2),
    minimum([C1,C2], C).
```

12.5.4 Explanation for the backward chainer

After a goal has been proved it is desirable to have the facility to examine the proof. We can arrange for this to happen by constructing the proof tree as the program executes. We need to add an argument for the proof into each of the rules used to execute the backward chainer. This is very much the same approach as we used for the recommended profession rule base.

```
deduce RHS :-
    backward_prove(RHS, Proof),
    see_proof(RHS, Proof).
backward_prove(RHS, fact(RHS)):-
    fact(RHS),
    explain([RHS,' is a known fact.']).
backward_prove(RHS, rule(RHS,Proof)):-
    (backward_rule if LHS then RHS),
    explain([RHS,' matches rule with LHS ',LHS]),
    backward_prove(LHS, Proof).
backward_prove(A and B, conjunction(Proof1,Proof2)):-
    backward_prove(A, Proof1),
    backward_prove(B, Proof2).
backward_prove(A, asked(A)):-
    askable(A),
    ask(A).
```

This produces for the "fish" example (I have laid this out in a readable form):

```
rule(
    cod has_property edible,
    conjunction(
        rule(
            cod isa fish,
            conjunction(
                fact(cod can swim),
                fact(cod has gills)
            )
            fact(cod found_in ocean)
        )
    )
)
```

As with the recommended profession example, we need to be able to translate this into something understandable. This is achieved here by using indentation, using the built-in predicate **tab**, to present the proof in a similar fashion to that above. In addition it writes where the rules and facts were used. The first rule initiates the explanation process by calling **output_proof** with a tab value of 0.

```
see_proof(RHS, Proof):-
    write('Do you want to see how '),
    write(RHS),
    write(' was deduced (y/n)?'),
    getyn(Ans),
```

```
    Ans = 121, /* 'y' */
    nl,
    output_proof(0,Proof).
output_proof(Tab, rule(RHS,LHS)):-
    tab(Tab),
    write(RHS),
    write(' was proved by proving the subgoal(s):'),nl,
    Tab1 is Tab + 8,
    output_proof(Tab1,LHS).
output_proof(Tab, conjunction(A,B)):-
    output_proof(Tab, A),
    tab(Tab),write('AND'),nl,
    output_proof(Tab, B).
output_proof(Tab, fact(A)):-
    tab(Tab),
    write(A),write(' - which is a fact.'),nl.
output_proof(Tab, asked(A)):-
    tab(Tab),
    write(A),write(' was given by the user.'),nl.
```

12.6 Conclusion

This chapter has introduced writing expert systems and inference engines in Prolog. It is possible to write very much more complex expert systems using Prolog. Furthermore, systems can be written that provide the inferencing and explanations for a variety of expert system methods within a single system. Such systems, called "shells", do not come with a specific knowledge or rule base, but will run with a variety of knowledge bases. Such a system is MIKE (micro interpreter for knowledge engineering), available from the Open University. This allows forward and backward chaining as well as a method of representing knowledge by so-called frames. MIKE will run with the Keylink interpreter and is introduced in the next chapter. For those wishing to study expert systems and knowledge engineering, MIKE is highly recommended.

CHAPTER THIRTEEN
MIKE

13.1 About MIKE

MIKE stands for micro interpreter for knowledge engineering. It was written by the Open University and version 2.03 has been supplied on the accompanying disk. Please note the conditions of use and copyright notice in the file **mike.pl** The Open University also supplies a study pack (code PD624) for MIKE, which contains tutorial text, a 180 minute VHS video and a 60 minute audiocassette. The study pack may be obtained from:

Learning Materials Sales Office
The Open University
PO Box 188
Milton Keynes
MK7 6DH
Tel: (+44) 01908 653338
Fax: (+44) 01908 653744

MIKE supports a variety of expert system approaches, including forward and backward chaining and the use of frames. It is ideal for teaching many of the components of the Scottish Higher concerned with knowledge representation and expert systems.

13.2 Using MIKE with Keylink Prolog

There are just two source code changes that must be made to the MIKE V2.03 source code to allow it to be successfully consulted and executed using Keylink Prolog. In **loadops.pl** change the line:

```
?- op(999,fx,[make_value,add_value]).
```

to:

```
?- op(999,fx,make_value).
?- op(999,fx,add_value).
```

In **engine2.pl** change the definition of the clause:

```
in_wm(prolog(X)):-
    !,
    X.
```

to:

```
in_wm(prolog(X)):-
    !,
    call(X).
```

You can consult MIKE with:

```
?- consult('mike.pl')
```

The **mike.pl** file has a series of **?- reconsult** directives that cause all the other MIKE files to be consulted. It expects all the other MIKE files to be in the current directory. Consulting **mike.pl** may take up to a minute or two. A convenient method for reducing this delay in future MIKE sessions is outlined in section 13.2.2.

These are all the changes needed for the PC or Nimbus user. However, you will almost certainly want to change the editor that is used in the **ed** predicate defined in file **mike.ini**.

13.2.1 Notes for Archimedes users

If you are an Archimedes user you will also need to change file names to suit the Archimedes. It is recommended that you change the dot extension (**.pl**) part of the DOS file names to underscore extension (**_pl**), for example **loadops.pl** becomes **loadops_pl**. You will need to find and change all occurrences of file names in MIKE to follow this convention. These occur in **mike.pl** and **mike.ini**. Take care, when consulting **mike_pl**, that the current directory is where the MIKE source files are. Note that any successfully consulted file is given the file type of Kprolog, that is from this point on it assumes the Prolog icon. All the MIKE files and knowledge bases are genuine Prolog files so they are legitimately given the Prolog file type. However, they cannot be understood by Prolog without MIKE being loaded. This is because MIKE defines many of its own operators in Prolog (see the file **loadops.pl**). Therefore it makes no sense to double click on, or drag into Prolog, any of the MIKE files except **mike_pl** (and in this case the current directory must be set to that of the MIKE sources). The same is true of the knowledge bases: these should always be loaded using MIKE's command **kb**.

13.2.2 Fast-loading MIKE

When you have successfully consulted MIKE you may wish to make a fast-loading version using **msave**. This will enable you to load MIKE in seconds rather than minutes. You should consult Chapter 14 for instructions on how to do this.

13.3 MIKE architecture

If you have read and tried the examples in the previous chapter you will find many of the concepts in MIKE familiar. As with the expert system shell we built in the previous chapter, MIKE is a Prolog program that allows various styles of rules to be defined and executed. We mostly work with MIKE by giving it commands and goals to the usual Prolog query prompt and terminating them with a full-stop.

As well as interacting with MIKE we can also call Prolog goals, including built-in predicates, directly.

MIKE consists of a working memory that consists of Prolog atoms, single quoted strings, lists and Prolog structures. We expect the working memory to contain the data that is relevant to the current state of play of the rule base that is being executed. We can think of it as a kind of scratch area or blackboard upon which various partial deductions and other results are placed.

MIKE also has a rule memory in which **if... then...** production rules are stored. This clearly forms the deductive component of the expert system that is to be executed.

Our effort in constructing an expert system in MIKE is directed at formulating these rules.

MIKE has an inference engine or, strictly speaking, it has several inference engines that allow it to apply the rules to the working memory and make deductions. Having several different inference engines allows it to apply its rules in fundamentally different ways, such as forward and backward chaining, which were discussed in the previous chapter.

MIKE has a command set that allows users to interrogate the state of the rule base and working memory. It also provides a range of diagnostic facilities so that we can test and debug our rule sets.

MIKE also has some rather advanced features such as frames, truth maintenance and demons, some of which will be discussed later in this chapter.

13.4 Running MIKE

The main MIKE file that must be consulted from Prolog is **mike.pl**. This contains a rule that loads the set of MIKE Prolog source files that constitute the MIKE system. If you look at the **mike.pl** file you will see the following rule:

```
loadmikesources :-
    write('Loading auxiliary MIKE files'),
    reconsult('loadops.pl'), write('loadops loaded'),nl,
    reconsult('engine1.pl'), write('engine1 loaded '),nl,
    reconsult('engine2.pl'), write('engine2 loaded'),nl,
    reconsult('fc_exec.pl'), write('fc_exec loaded'),nl,
    reconsult('io.pl'), write('io loaded'),nl,
    reconsult('util.pl'), write('util loaded'),nl,
    reconsult('findall.pl'), write('findall loaded'),nl,
    reconsult('browse.pl'), write('browse loaded'),nl,
    reconsult('worlds.pl'), write('worlds loaded'),nl,
    reconsult('xtend.pl'), write('xtend loaded'). /* Use
        xtend.pl for personal extensions */
```

Each of these files provides part of the functionality of MIKE, for example the inference engines are defined in **engine1.pl** and **engine2.pl**. Even if you are not going to use all of MIKE's functionality it is important to load all of the files. So do not be tempted to edit **mike.pl** or any other of the MIKE source files.

All of MIKE's source files should be kept in a single directory. If you are using DOS or RiscOS you must make this the current directory.

Consult the file by using the query:

```
?- consult('mike.pl').
```

or, if you are using Windows, use the menu sequence File/Open, then use the file dialogue to go to MIKE's directory and select **mike.pl**.

As MIKE loads it reports on the successful loading of each source file and then displays a MIKE copyright banner.

All of MIKE's examples are in files with the extension **.kb**, for knowledge base. On RiscOS the files will terminate with **_kb**. As an example we will run the tea-making knowledge base. Enter the following query:

```
?- kb 'teamakin.kb'.
```

Notice the space between **kb** and the file name, the use of single quotes around the file name and the full-stop at the end.

MIKE will output a set of statistics concerning the knowledge base that it has just loaded and you will again be faced with the normal Prolog query prompt.

We can ask MIKE to display the current contents of working memory by entering:

```
?- wm.
```

You will see that MIKE currently has nothing in its working memory. This is a normal state when a knowledge base has not yet been executed and no working memory entries have been explicitly provided by you.

The tea-making example is a forward chainer, and we can invoke the forward chaining inference engine with the MIKE command **fc**. Enter the following query:

```
?- fc.
```

MIKE will invoke the forward chainer on the current knowledge base and you will immediately see the results, which consist of a set of instructions on how to make a cup of tea.

We can interrogate the contents of working memory again with the query:

```
?- wm.
```

This time you will see that there are 10 working memory entries. All of these entries, bar one, describe a state during the process of making a cup of tea that MIKE will have used when determining what to do next. The working memory entry **start** is rather special and is discussed later in the chapter when we take a closer look at using MIKE for forward chaining.

13.5 Backward chaining

The syntax of a MIKE backward chaining rule is:

```
rule <rule name> backward
if <condition1>
    & <condition2>
    & ...
then <conclusion>.
```

Notice that the rule is terminated with a full-stop. **rule, backward, if, &** and **then** are all symbols that MIKE recognizes. These have been declared as operators in the MIKE source file **loadops.pl** using the Prolog built-in **op/3**.

The rule name is an arbitrary Prolog atom that the knowledge engineer uses to label rules.

The various conditions that must be satisfied (the antecedents) are separated by logical conjunctions, represented in MIKE by the **&** symbol. We can also use disjunctions which are represented by the symbol **or**.

The conditions may be as follows:

<working memory pattern>
This is something to be matched against working memory, for example an atom such as red or a string such as "light is red", Prolog lists and struc-

135

tures are also valid; these may contain variables, as in `colour(X)`.

– <working memory pattern>

This is a negation of a working memory pattern, i.e. exactly the same as above but the condition must not match a working memory element.

deduce <working memory pattern>

This is similar to the above, but in the case the working memory pattern is expected to match by invoking rules rather than matching directly on a working memory element, hence the keyword **deduce**, i.e. the working memory pattern is expected to be deduced. We sometimes refer to this as triggering further backward chaining.

prolog(<goal>)

This enables us to pass an arbitrary goal to Prolog. It is commonly used to perform arithmetic, which MIKE does not support directly. So we might calculate a volume, for example, with `prolog(V is H*W*L)`.

query <query template>

This enables us to ask the user of the knowledge base a question as the knowledge base is executing. MIKE recognizes a variety of templates that can be used to get yes/no type answers or text from the user, or even display a list of options for the user to select from.

Conclusion:

<working memory pattern> of a rule is proved when all the left-hand side conditions are satisfied. It is just simply proved, i.e. shown to be true, it is *not* added to working memory.

Consider, for example, the creatures knowledge base, `cr_b.kb`. This uses a set of backward chaining rules to determine the type of animal when the user gives values to various animal characteristics. Many of the rules, quite naturally, have left-hand sides that consist of user queries and conclusions that give the user's response:

```
rule body_covering backward
    if query 'What is the body_covering? (hair/feathers/
    other/unknown) '
        receives_answer X
    & prolog(X=Y)
    then body_covering(Y).
```

This rule, called **body_covering**, uses a query to ask the user what type of body covering the animal has. This particular form of query template expects the user to type an arbitrary atom that is instantiated to the variable that is the argument to **receives_answer**. The text of the question tries to prompt the user into supplying an answer that is going to be meaningful to the knowledge base.

An example that uses deduce is:

```
rule mammal_1 backward
    if deduce body_covering(hair)
    then mammal.
```

i.e. if a rule or rules can be invoked that conclude that the body covering is hair, then this rule can conclude that the animal is a mammal.

A rule using several instances of deduce is:

```
rule feeding_type_1 backward
    if deduce mammal
        & deduce eats(meat)
    then feeding_type(carnivore).
```

The semantics or meaning of this should be clear.

Briefly have a look at the entire creatures knowledge base using an editor or print it out for reference. Ignore anything to do with explanation for the moment.

Run the example by loading MIKE into Prolog and then loading the creatures knowledge base with the query:

```
?- kb 'cr_b.kb'.
```

We need to invoke the backward chainer explicitly by using deduce followed by the conclusion that we wish the backward chainer to reach. For example:

```
?- deduce species(X).
```

This is an example dialogue:

```
What is the body_covering? (hair/feathers/other/unknown)
    ==> |: feathers.
What does it feed its young on? (milk/other/unknown)
    ==> |: unknown.
How does it move? (flies/swims/walks/unknown)
    ==> |: swims.
What is the colour? (tawny/black_and_white/other/
    unknown)
    ==> |: black_and_white.
X = penguin
```

Exercise 13a: choosing a pub

Write a simple backward chaining expert system that determines which pub to go to. Try to structure the questions into determining answers that can be used in several rules. For example, ask "What kind of drink do you like?", rather than asking "Do you like real ale?" in one place and "Do you like spirits?" in another. You may like to take a copy of the creatures knowledge base and modify it. This gives you a much greater chance of getting the syntax correct.

You should be able to start the system with the query:

```
?- deduce recommended_pub(X).
```

Here are some ideas for rules; refine and expand these, but try to get a small knowledge base working first.

```
likes loud rock music, real ale, money no object =>
dog and trumpet

must be cheap, likes students => union bar

likes irish music, mixed company and drinking guinness
=> eight bells

likes live music, young company and anything to drink
=> silver sword

likes refined company, drinking spirits, dislikes
music, money no object => de vere
```

13.6 Providing "canned" explanation to "Why?"

A simple explanation can be provided to questions of the "Why?" variety via the **explained_by** keyword. Take the **body_covering** rule from the creatures knowledge base:

```
rule body_covering backward

    if query 'What is the body_covering? (hair/feathers/
    other/unknown) '

        receives_answer X

    & prolog(X=Y)

    then body_covering(Y).
```

We can provide a canned explanation for why this rule is being invoked with the following:

```
'What is the body_covering? (hair/feathers/other/unknown) '

explained_by

    ['If the body covering is known to be hair', nl, 'then it
    can be concluded that the creature is a mammal.', nl, 'If
    it is feathers, then the creature is a bird'].
```

What comes before the **explained_by** keyword must match the query text exactly. I call the explanation "canned" because there is no intelligence to it whatsoever, it is simply text to be regurgitated at the user word for word when the user types **why**. However, given its simplicity, it can transform a system from being totally unhelpful to being quite user friendly when seen from the user's perspective.

138

Now when the user is asked the question:

What is the body_covering? (hair/feathers/other/unknown)

and the user enters:

why.

the canned explanation text will be displayed and MIKE will then wait for the answer.

Exercise 13b

Provide an explanation of the "canned" variety to your pub knowledge base.

13.7 Forward chaining

The syntax of a forward chaining rule is:

```
rule <rule name> forward
if <condition1>
    & <condition2>
    & ...
then <action1>
    & <action2>
    &...
    & <action n>.
```

Notice that instead of a conclusion we have any number of actions that will typically assert something into working memory.

The conditions may be as follows:

<working memory pattern>
This is something to be matched against working memory, as described for backward chaining.

— <working memory pattern>
This is a negation of a working memory pattern.

deduce <working memory pattern>
We can trigger backward chaining from a forward chaining rule!

prolog(<goal>)
This enables us to pass an arbitrary goal to Prolog.

query <query template>
This is enables us to ask the user questions, as described for backward chaining rules.

Right-hand side actions can:
modify working memory:

```
add <working memory pattern>

remove <working memory pattern>
```

provide output:

```
announce <announcement list>
```

perform arithmetic:

```
<var> := <arithmetic expression>
```

query the user:

```
query <query template>

receives_answer <variable>

ask_menu(<object>, <attribute>, <list>)
```

execute Prolog goals:

```
prolog(<goal1>, <goal2>,...)
```

terminate execution:

```
halt
```

13.8 Running the forward chaining inference engine

The forward chainer can be started with:

```
?- fc.
```

This erases the contents of working memory using the MIKE defined goal **initialise**. Then MIKE seeds working memory with the symbol **start** using the goal **add start**. This is a symbol that we can use in our knowledge bases to recognize the starting point of execution. Forward chaining is then commenced using the MIKE command **go**.

The cycle that the forward chainer makes should be familiar from the previous chapter, but MIKE's version is rather more advanced in that it uses something called conflict resolution to select rules for firing:

```
repeat
    match the rules against the contents of working
      memory, those that match form the conflict set.
    select a single rule from the conflict set using a
      conflict resolution strategy.
    execute the RHS actions of the selected rule.
until no matching rules or halt
```

MIKE has three strategies for picking the most suitable rule to fire, otherwise known as conflict resolution.

- Refractoriness: once a rule has fired give it low priority for subsequent firing.

- Recency: give priority to rules that match on recently added working memory elements.
- Specificity: give priority to rules with the most left-hand side conditions.

MIKE's default behaviour is refractoriness, recency then specificity.

A forward chaining version of the creatures knowledge base can be found in **cr_f1.kb**. Here are a few of its rules:

```
rule mammal_1 forward
    if [creature, body_covering, hair]
    then add [creature, mammal, yes].
rule bird_2 forward
    if [creature, motion, flies]
        & [creature, reproduction, eggs]
    then add [creature, bird, yes].
```

Here our working memory elements are Prolog lists that we are using to store **<object>,<attribute>,<value>** triplets. We could just as well used a Prolog structure for the same purpose. The important point is that the rules must be consistent in matching on and adding to the working memory.

This version does not ask for information from the user. It expects all the necessary information to be in working memory already. This means that to run the system we must first seed working memory with sufficient working memory elements to identify a creature and then use **go** to start the chainer, rather than **fc**, which would remove the working memory elements we have just provided! You need to be rather careful with your input. Notice that I have used one of the tracing facilities of MIKE with the command:

```
?- tracing(5).
```

This allows us to see the changes that are made to working memory as they happen.

See over for a complete dialogue.

The forward chainer is automatically able to provide explanations of how conclusions have been arrived at. We use the **how** command followed by a working memory pattern, as with:

```
?- how [creature,species,zebra].
[creature,species,zebra] was concluded from species_4
with the following premises
    [creature,feeding_type,ungulate] &
    [creature,colour,black_and_white]
yes
```

?- kb 'cr_f1.kb'.
New knowledge base loaded.

MIKE OPTIONS   USEFUL COMMANDS   STATUS/COUNT
TMS...................... tms_on.   tms_off.   off
RETE..................... rete_on.   rete_off.   off
Rules.................... show rules. describe R.   15
Frames................... browse.   describe F.   0
Working memory elements.. wm. cf.   0
Uncertainty paradigm..... certainty.   threshold.   standard
Current knowledge base... kb '<filename>'.   cr_f1.kb

Current conflict resolution strategy (in order) is:
[refractoriness,recency,specificity,lhsthreshold,cfstrength]
with a left-hand-side certainty threshold of 0.2.
----
yes
?- add [creature,body_covering,hair].
yes
?- add [creature,eats,grass].
yes
?- add [creature,colour,black_and_white].
yes
?- wm.
The current contents of working memory are the following:
      [creature,body_covering,hair]
      [creature,eats,grass]

```
            [creature,colour,black_and_white]
A total of 3 current working memory elements were found.
yes
?- tracing(5).
+ 5: show new working memory elements or frame changes is    currently enabled
yes
?- go.
New working memory elements or frame changes are:
[creature,mammal,yes]
New working memory elements or frame changes are:
[creature,feeding_type,ungulate]
New working memory elements or frame changes are:
[creature,species,zebra]
New working memory elements or frame changes are:
halt
yes
?- wm.
The current contents of working memory are the following:
            [creature,body_covering,hair]
            [creature,eats,grass]
            [creature,colour,black_and_white]
            [creature,mammal,yes]
            [creature,feeding_type,ungulate]
            [creature,species,zebra]
A total of 6 current working memory elements were found.
yes
```

Exercise 13c

Modify the pubs example to be a forward chainer. Use the same working memory representation as for the creatures example, i.e. **[person, likes, loud_music]**.

13.9 Using menus

We use **MIKE**'s ask_menu/3 function to display options to the user. For example, if we have the rule:

```
rule get_symptom forward
if
    diagnosing
    & [current_patient, P]
then
ask_menu(P,exhibits_symptom,[sneezing,↲
coughing,headache,spots]).
```

When this rule fires the user is presented with a menu of the items in the list and may select any number of them; for each choice a triple of the form [P, exhibits_symptom, S] is put into working memory.

This rule is in the file symptom.pl. Here is an example of its use:

```
?- kb 'symptom.kb'.
```

(MIKE displays its status screen)

```
?- add diagnosing.
yes
?- add [current_patient,john].
yes
?- go.
*********************************
1 - sneezing
2 - coughing
3 - headache
4 - spots
Choose the items from the menu by typing the correspond-
ing number(s). Separate numbers with commas e.g. 1,3,5.
REMEMBER to use a FULL STOP ('.') at the end
==> |: 1,3.
New working memory elements or frame changes are:
New working memory elements or frame changes are:
halt
yes
```

```
?- wm.
The current contents of working memory are the following:
    diagnosing
    [current_patient,john]
    [john,exhibits_symptom,sneezing]
    [john,exhibits_symptom,headache]
A total of 4 current working memory elements were found.
yes
```

Exercise 13d

Modify the forward chaining version of the pubs knowledge base to ask for the user's preferences via menus.

A good example of a more advanced use of menus can be found in the file **cr_f2.kb**. This example goes through an information-gathering phase at the start of execution, which is controlled by keeping certain elements in working memory. The initialization rule is:
rule initialisation forward

```
if start

then remove start
    & add attribute_list(body_covering, [hair,
    feathers, other])
    & add attribute_list(colour, [tawny,
    black_and_white, other])
    & add attribute_list(eats, [meat, grass, other])
    & add attribute_list(eyes, [point_forward,
    point_sideways])
    & add attribute_list(feeds_young_on, [milk,
    other])
    & add attribute_list(feet, [claws, hoofs, other])
    & add attribute_list(legs_and_neck, [long, short])
    & add attribute_list(marking, [dark_spots,
    black_stripes, other])
    & add attribute_list(motion, [flies, swims,
    walks])
    & add attribute_list(reproduction, [eggs, other])
    & add attribute_list(teeth, [pointed, blunt])
    & add get_attribute
    & strategy [recency, specificity].
```

It uses the symbol **start** to recognize the start of execution and initializes a set of working memory elements of the form:

`attribute_list(<attribute name> <list of attribute values>)`

to store the set of attributes that the user may give values for. It also puts the element `get_attribute` into working memory to flag the fact that it is in the process of collecting the attribute information from the user. Finally, it changes the conflict resolution strategy to remove refractoriness that is not required, and would be entirely inappropriate, during the information-gathering stage.

The next rule checks to see whether it is in the information-gathering stage by looking for the symbol `get_attribute` in working memory and then uses **announce** to prompt the user for the attribute for which a value is required.

```
rule get_attribute forward
    if get_attribute
    then announce ['What attribute do you want to provide
    a value for? ', nl]
        & ask_menu(creature, attribute, [body_covering,
        colour, eats, eyes, feeds_young_on, feet,
        legs_and_neck, marking, motion, reproduction,
        teeth, thats_all])
        & remove get_attribute.
```

The **ask_menu/3** call will display a menu of the selectable attributes. When the user selects **body_covering**, for example, a working memory element of the form:

`[creature, attribute, body_covering]`

is asserted. The following rule looks for such working memory patterns and when it finds one it looks up the corresponding list of attribute values via the **attribute_list(X, Y)** call.

```
rule get_value forward
    if [creature, attribute, X]
        & — [creature, attribute, thats_all]
        & attribute_list(X,Y)
    then announce ['What is the value of ', X, '?', nl]
        & ask_menu(creature, X, Y)
        & remove [creature, attribute, X]
        & add get_attribute.
```

It then uses **ask_menu** with the attribute name and list to prompt the user for the required value.

The final information-gathering rule looks for **thats_all** (this is displayed via the **get_attribute** rule), removes it from working memory, adds the element **identify**, which the remainder of the rule base will recognize and finally restores the conflict resolution strategy to its default values.

```
rule continue forward
    if [creature, attribute, thats_all]
    then remove [creature, attribute, thats_all]
        & add identify
        & strategy [refractoriness, recency, specificity].
```

The execution is being controlled very precisely by careful use of **add** and **remove** to allow the desired rule to fire. This may seem a bit tricky, but given the fact that we have no direct control over the flow of the control it is the only way we can get the desired effect.

13.10 Frames and classes

A class or a frame is a structure that groups together a set of attributes under a single unique class name. This is very much like the idea of a record in a database that groups together a set of fields into a table that has a unique table name. We use the word class to mean the definition of the frame rather than a particular instance of it. A class is the generic description of a frame, whereas an instance is a specific example of a particular class. We call the attributes of a class the slots.

An example of a class is:

```
person subclass_of_living_thing with
    name:unknown,
    sex:unknown,
    age:unknown,
    likes_cats:true.
```

This has the slots **name, sex, age** and **likes_cats**. Notice that the attribute names and attribute values are separated by colons, and each slot description is separated with a comma. When we declare a class, as in this example, we have the opportunity to provide default values for the slots that will be used in the case of a particular instance if that instance does not provide its own. An example of an instance of this class is:

```
person_1 instance_of person with
    name:jane,
    sex:female,
    age:90,
    likes_cats:false.
```

We can access frame slot values using the following MIKE syntax:

```
?- the sex of person_1 is X.
X = female
```

We can instantiate a variable to an instance of a class by using the **instance_of** operator:

147

```
?- X instance_of person.

X = person_1.
```

We can qualify which instance or instances we require by specifying values for the slots, as in:

```
?- X instance_of person,
    the age of X is 90.

X = person_1.
```

We can also declare a subclass of an existing class that automatically inherits the slots of its parent class and adds new slots that are only relevant to the subclass. For example:

```
teacher subclass_of person with
    subject: unknown.
```

An instance of this may use the newly declared slot as well as the parent slots:

```
teacher_1 instance_of teacher with
    name:jim,
    sex:male,
    age:45,
    subject:computing.
```

This instance and its slots may be accessed in exactly the same way as shown above:

```
?- the name of teacher_1 is X.

X = jim
```

Not only are the slots inherited by the subclass, but the default values are also inherited from the parent class:

```
?- the likes_cats of teacher_1 is X.

    X = true
```

We can change the value of a slot using the keyword "note". For example:

```
?- note the likes_cats of teacher_1 is false.
```

Frames can be accessed within both the left- and right-hand side of rules. For example:

```
rule i_like_you forward
    if X instance_of teacher
        & the likes_cats of X is true
        & the name of X is Name
    then
        announce ['I like you ',Name, '.'].
```

This would give the output:

```
I like you jim.
```

The note facility could be used on the right-hand side of a rule to change the value of a slot.

13.11 Facet types

Frame slots can have not only attribute–value pairs, such as we have seen examples of, but also facet–filler pairs within each slot. The value–attribute pair is in fact just one of many possible types of facet.

13.11.1 value

We have already met this, for example:

```
bike instance_of vehicle with
    wheels: 2,
    uses: ['keeping fit', travelling].
```

Or we can be more specific in that we are supplying values for:

```
bike instance_of vehicle with
    wheels: [value: 2],
    uses: [value: ['keeping fit', travelling]].
```

13.11.2 type (optional)

type restricts the type of object that can fill a slot. Here **type** is being used in the same way as we use it for describing variables in a computer language such as Pascal. Types can be restricted to integers, atoms or to domains supplied as lists, for example:

```
car subclass_of vehicle with
    wheels:
        [value: 4,
        type: integer].
escort instance_of car with
    seats:
        [value: 4,
         type: integer],
    uses: [pleasure, work].
```

The following queries will generate warning messages:

```
?- note the wheels of escort is five.
?- note the seats of escort is four.
```

The first query generates a warning because the type restriction on wheels is inherited from the subclass declaration for car. The second query generates a warning because of the typing given in the creation of the instance **escort**.

13.11.3 cardinality (optional)

In normal use cardinality just means the number of. In this context the cardinality determines how many filler values a slot may have. For example:

```
car subclass_of vehicle with
    can_reverse:
        [value: yes,
            type: [yes, no],
            cardinality: 1],
    use:
        [value: [work, pleasure],
        cardinality: 1-2].
```

=> `can_reverse` must be exactly one of {yes, no} and **use** can have up to two values, but note that the domain has not been given.

Given an instance of car, for example:

```
escort instance_of car.
```

Then the following produces a warning:

```
?- note the use of escort is [work,pleasure,racing].
```

as the cardinality constraint is being broken.

13.11.4 inheritance (default supersede)

inheritance is used to specify how we want domains to be treated by subclasses. It allows us to choose between having the domains of the subclass and the parent classes merged or entirely superseded.

If **inheritance** for a subclass is **supersede**, then the domain of possible fillers for an instance of that subclass replace those values that might be inherited. If **inheritance** is **merge**, the domain of possible fillers for an instance is merged with the inherited domain values.

```
car subclass_of vehicle with
    can_reverse:
        [value: yes,
        type: [yes, no],
        cardinality: 1],
    use:
        [value: [work, pleasure],
        inheritance: merge,
        cardinality: 1-5].
taxi subclass_of car with
    colour: black,
```

```
use:
    [value: hire,
     inheritance: merge].
car67 instance_of taxi with
    seats: 4.
```

The following query shows the result of the **merge** inheritance, which combines the possible values for the slot "use":

```
?- all use of car67 are What.
What = [work, pleasure, hire]
```

13.11.4 change_rule

A slot can have some executable code associated with it (commonly called a demon). This code will be given in normal MIKE/Prolog syntax and is invoked in particular situations that have proved to be useful.

We can arrange to have demons executed automatically in one of two situations. A demon can be invoked when a slot is changed (i.e. by use of **note**) or when it is accessed. We need to supply a **change_rule** slot for the former and an **access_rule** slot for the latter. Whenever we supply **change_rule** or **access_rule** slots for a frame, then the code in the **change_rule** slot is automatically executed by the inference engine whenever this slot is changed. The code in the **access_rule** slot is automatically executed whenever this slot is accessed. These enable us to keep our code very declarative as we do not have to write any code for testing these situations, we simply declare what is to happen as properties of the frame. When a change is made to the filler of a slot using the **note** operator, MIKE's inference engine looks for the presence of a change rule to be invoked as a result of this change and fires it. Similarly, when a slot is accessed, MIKE's inference engine looks for the presence of an access rule and, if there is one, the inference engine fires it.

A change rule or access rule is declared as a facet just like a type or cardinality declaration. It can also be inherited from the parent class. A change rule looks and behaves like a normal forward chaining rule. When a change rule succeeds, its right-hand part is executed silently. When it fails, a warning is given.

A very simple use of a change rule would be to provide warnings when illegal values are assigned to a slot.

An extra feature is provided that allows the object being changed to be accessed within the change rule. This is achieved by the use of the object name **?self**. **?self** means that the name of the object is substituted in the rule wherever **?self** is used, for example:

```
taxi subclass_of car with
    status:
```

```
        [type: [for_hire,not_for_hire,hired],
        cardinality: 1],
    next_service:
        [type: integer],
    mileage:
        [value : integer,
        change_rule :
            (if
                the mileage of ?self is Mileage
            &
                the next_service of ?self is NextService
            &
                Mileage > NextService
            then
                note the status of ?self is not_for_hire
            )
        ].
```

Here the change rule checks to see if the mileage of the taxi has taken it beyond its next service. If it has we force the status of the taxi to not for hire. We can declare an instance of taxi in the normal way:

```
car67 instance_of taxi with
    status: for_hire,
    next_service : 12000,
    mileage : 11999.
```

For example, suppose that we wish to say that **car67** now has a mileage of **12030**:

```
?- note the mileage of car67 is 12030.
    yes.
?- describe car67.
car67 instance_of taxi with
    status: not_for_hire
    next_service : 12000,
    mileage : 12030.
yes.
```

The left-hand side of change rules can consist entirely of the atom true. This is so that it can always succeed if required.

13.11.5 access_rule

Access rules backward chain in order to provide a value for a slot. They use the normal syntax for backward chaining rules (one goal on the right-hand side). The conclusion is normally deduced and not inserted into frame memory. However, the keyword **make_value** can be used to assign a slot value destructively from the right-hand side of an access rule, for example:

```
bullet subclass_of missile with
    kinetic_energy :
        [value : unknown,
        access_rule :
            (if
                the speed of ?self is Speed &
                the mass of ?self is Mass &
                prolog(KE is 0.5 * Mass * Speed * Speed)
            then
                make_value KE)].
slug45 instance_of bullet with
    mass : 0.20,
    speed : 1500.
```

In the declaration of slug45 there is no slot for kinetic energy, but it inherits a method for calculating the value from its parent class. **make_value** has been used on the right-hand side of the access rule therefore the frame itself will be updated to contain this new value.

```
?- the kinetic_energy of slug45 is What.
What = 225000
?- describe slug45.
slug45 instance_of bullet with

    mass : 0.2,
    speed : 1500,
    kinetic_energy : 225000.
yes.
```

If we do not wish to update the frame with the kinetic energy value permanently, we can simply calculate the value in the right-hand side of the access rule, for example:

```
bullet subclass_of missile with
    kinetic_energy :
        [value : unknown,
        access_rule :
            (if
                the speed of ?self is Speed &
                the mass of ?self is Mass &
                prolog(KE is 0.5 * Mass * Speed * Speed)
```

```
                then
                    the kinetic_energy of ?self is KE)].
    slug45 instance_of bullet with
        mass : 0.20,
        speed : 1500.
```

When we use this definition, we get a value for kinetic energy when we access that slot, but we do not when we describe the object as the kinetic energy slot is not a permanent part of the frame:

```
?- the kinetic_energy of slug45 is What.
What = 225000
?- describe slug45.
slug45 instance_of bullet with
    mass : 0.2,
    speed : 1500.
yes.
```

13.12 Flush toilet simulation

This example knowledge base is in the file **toilet.kb**. There are only three elements: **float1, tank1** and **pipe1. pipe1** starts off with a flow rate of 5, **tank1** starts off at level 0. As the float rises, the flow rate decreases. Flow rate is simply (hard wired) to be **5 - (FloatHeight//2)** This example encodes the behaviour of the components of the cistern quite declaratively, and when running it provides a simulation of the behaviour of a cistern filling. The effect of one component on another is achieved by the use of change rules.

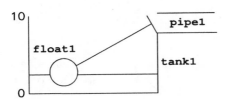

The following are simple declarations of some of the components.

```
    tank1 instance_of tank with
        height: 5,
        width: 4,
        depth: 3,
        regulator: float1.
    float1 instance_of float with
```

```
    arm_length: 4,
    regulated_inlet: pipe1.
pipe1 instance_of pipe with
    thickness: 5,
    comes_from: mains_supply,
    goes_to: tank1,
    flow_rate: 5.
pipe subclass_of flow_through_device with
    material: copper.
```

A change rule is included in the following description of the tank, which provides for a simple drawing of the level of the tank to be made.

```
tank subclass_of vessel with
    level :
        [value: L,
        change_rule : (if the regulator of ?self is Reg
        then prolog(draw_image('level of tank 1',L)) &
        note the height of Reg is L)].
```

The change rule for the float calculates the new flow rate for the inlet.

```
float subclass_of regulating_feedback_valves with
    arm_length: AL,
    regulated_inlet: P,
    height :
        [value: H,
        change_rule: (if the regulated_inlet of ?self is
        Inlet then prolog(NewFlowRate is 5 - (H//2)) &
        note the flow_rate of Inlet is NewFlowRate)].
```

The first rule clears **start** symbol from working memory, then dynamically alters the conflict resolution strategy so that only refractoriness is used (and not specificity or recency). It initializes the tank level to zero and sets the tank filling.

```
rule init forward
    if
        start /* special symbol that is always in WM at
start */
    then
        remove start &
        strategy [refractoriness] &
        note the level of tank1 is 0 &
        add tank_filling.
```

The next rule is used to stop the forward chainer when the level of the tank exceeds 9. This restores the conflict resolution strategy to the default values and halts.

```
rule stop_it forward
    if
        tank_filling &
        the level of tank1 > 9 /* will eventually reach
this */
    then
        strategy [refractoriness, recency, specificity] &
        halt .
```

The filling rule, which follows, uses the level of **tank1** and flow rate of **pipe1** to calculate the new level of **tank1**.

```
rule filling forward
    if
        tank_filling &
        the level of tank1 is L &
        the flow_rate of pipe1 is R
    then
        prolog(NewLevel is L + R) &
        note the level of tank1 is NewLevel. /* this
            triggers change_rule */
```

The simulation can be started in the usual way for a forward chainer with:

```
?- fc.
```

What happens at this point is as follows:

- The **init** rule fires, which sets the level of **tank1** to zero and sets the tank filling.
- The **filling** rule fires, with the level of **tank1** = 0 and flow rate of **pipe1** = 5. **NewLevel** is calculated to be 5. The new level of **tank1** is noted; this fires **tank1**'s change rule.
- **tank1**'s change rule draws the height and notes the height of the float, which fires the **float1**'s change rule.
- **float1**'s change rule calculates and notes the flow rate of the pipe.
- The **filling** rule fires . . .

This continues until the conditions are such that the **stop_it** rule will fire and halt the forward chainer.

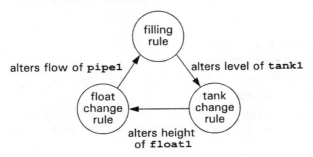

13.13 Conclusion

This chapter has attempted to introduce the main features of MIKE, which includes backward and forward chaining and the use of frames. There is rather more to MIKE than has been included in this chapter, and the reader is encouraged to obtain the study pack from the Open University, which is highly recommended.

Built-in predicates

<, >, =<, >=, ==, =\=

These are infix operators that perform an arithmetical comparison of what is on the left- and right-hand sides of the operator. They succeed if the left-hand side is less than, greater than, less than or equal, greater than or equal, equal or not equal respectively. Notice that these operators force evaluation of their arguments, unlike other comparison operators, e.g. =, ==, \==. Examples are:

```
?- 5 > 7.
no
?- 12 + 8 > 19.
yes
?- 3 * 3 >= 9.
yes
?- 4 + 2 =:= 6.
yes
?- 4 + 1 =\= 6.
yes
```

@<, @=<, @>, @>=

These predicates test standard order relationships between two terms. They test less than, less than or equal, greater than and greater than or equal respectively. In the standard ordering of terms variables are less than numbers, which are less than atoms, which are less than compound terms. Within these an older variable is less than a younger variable. Numbers are in numeric order; when a float is the same as an integer, the integer comes first. Atoms are in ASCII collating sequence order. Compound terms are ordered by arity, then by functor, then by standard order of components.

Examples are:

```
?- fred @< george.
yes
?- a(1,2) @< a(2,2).
yes.
```

<<, >>

These are infix operators that shift the bit-pattern representing the number to the left of the operator left (<<) or right (>>) by the number of bits specified to the right of the operator. For example:

```
?- X is (1 << 1). /* shift left 0001 1 bit gives 0010 */
X = 2
?- X is (4 >> 2). /* shift right 0100 2 bits gives 0001 */
X = 1
```

X = Y

This is an infix operator that tests whether the terms either side of it can be matched. Terms can be matched if:

1. they are identical, or
2. any variables in both terms can be instantiated in such a way that the two terms become identical.

In the following examples, all variables are initially uninstantiated:

```
?- X = Y.
X = _28102
Y = _28102
yes
?- father( X, george) = father( william, Y).
X = william
Y= george
yes
```

X = .. Y

This predicate is known as **univ**. It is useful for constructing terms from lists or for decomposing a term into a list of its parts. **X =.. Y** succeeds if **Y** is a list comprising the principal functor of **x** followed by its arguments. Examples are:

```
?- rides(dirk,yamaha) =.. X.
X = [rides,dirk,yamaha]
yes
?- X =.. [married,charlie,di]
X = married(charlie,di)
yes
```

X = = Y, \= =

This a stricter test of equality than =. For **x** == **y** to succeed not only must **x** and **y** be unifiable, but corresponding variables in the terms must be the same. The complementary relation \== will be true where == fails. For example:

```
?- X == Y.
no
?- X == X.
yes
?- t1(X,Y) == t1(X,Z).
no
?- X \== Y.
yes
```

X ^ Y

This is equivalent to "there exists an X such that Y is true", and is therefore equivalent to calling **Y**. Provision of ^ is made to give compatibility with other Prolog systems.

abolish(X)

This retracts all clauses with heads having a given functor. For example:

```
?- abolish(blue).
```

retracts all clauses whose heads have functor blue regardless of the arity.

abolish(X,A)

This retracts all clauses with heads having functor X and arity A. For example:

```
?- abolish(blue,2).
```

Will retract all clauses with functor **blue** of arity 2.

abort

This abandons the current solution process and returns control to the top-level interpreter.

arg(N,Term,A)

This succeeds if A is the Nth argument in Term. It can be used either for extracting arguments from a term or for instantiating a term's arguments. For example:

```
?- arg(1,(paragraph(sentence(word))),A).
A = sentence(word)
yes
?- arg(2,married(charlie,X),di).
X = di
yes
```

assert(X), asserta(X), assertz(X)

These three predicates enable the addition of clauses to Prolog's database, acting in the same way, except that **asserta** will add the clause to the start of the database, while **assert** and **assertz** will add the clause at the end of the database. Examples are:

```
?- asserta(swims(fish)).
```

will add the clause **swims(fish).** at the start of the database, while

```
?- assertz(swims(fish)).
```

will add **swims(fish).** to the end of the database. Note that in a subgoal **asserta(X)**, **X** must already be instantiated to something representing a clause.

When we say that clauses are added to start of the database, we mean the start of clauses with the same functor as the clause we are adding.

atom(X)

The goal **atom(X)** succeeds if **X** is currently instantiated to an atom. Examples are:

```
?- atom(23).
no
?- atom(apples).
yes
?- atom(X).
no
```

atomic(X)

The goal **atomic(X)** succeeds if X is currently instantiated to an atom or a number. Examples:

```
?- atomic(23).
yes
?- atomic(apples).
yes
?- atomic(X).
no
```

call(X)

The argument X should be instantiated to a term that can be interpreted as a goal: **call(X)** will then succeed if an attempt to satisfy its argument succeeds. For example, given the facts:

```
falcon(kestrel).
goal(falcon(X)).
then:
?- goal(X),call(X).
X = falcon(kestrel)
yes
```

cleardb

This clears Prolog's internal database of all facts and rules. For example:

```
?- assertz(likes(seal,fish)). /* Enter clause to db... */
yes
?- cleardb. /* ...clear db... */
yes
?- listing. /* ...db now empty */
yes
```

clock(X)

This instantiates X to the number of seconds of CPU time used.

close_log (PC only)

This stops logging the Prolog session and closes the log file opened using **log(F)**. The file will be automatically closed on any graceful exit from Prolog.

consult(F)

This allows a file containing Prolog clauses to be read into the internal database. For example:

```
?- consult(test).
```

will read in all Prolog clauses in the file **test**. A second use of `consult` will result in all new clauses in the second file being appended to the database. However, any clauses in the database with the same head and arity as any in the file being consulted will be replaced by those new clauses. All clauses forming a single rule should be contiguous in a file; if they are not then Keylink Prolog will issue a warning: **Clauses not together in rule: predname/arity**. Use of the "pseudofile" **user**, i.e.

```
?- consult( user).
```

will result in clauses typed by the user at the terminal being read directly to the database by Prolog, until the user types **?- seen.**, at which point the **?-** query prompt will be displayed, and anything typed at the terminal will be interpreted as a query.

exceptions(X)

This is used to change and examine the exception-raising status of the interpreter. The default behaviour is for an exception to be raised when an error is made in a query, resulting in error messages being displayed, for example:

```
?- name(X,X).
!! Type error in argument 2
!! Goal is: name(_32559,_32560)
!! String expected
!! Execution aborted
```

Such an error results in the execution of the current goal being cancelled. Exception raising can be turned off by using:

```
?- exceptions(off).
```

and reinstated via:

```
?- exceptions(on).
```

The current status can be examined via:

```
?- exceptions(X).

X = on
```

Where exception raising is turned off and an error is made in using a predicate, the predicate in question will silently fail, that is no error messages will be displayed and execution will continue at the nearest backtrack point.

exists(F)

This succeeds if the file F exists in the current directory.

fail

This goal always fails, causing backtracking to occur, and can therefore be used to generate multiple solutions to a goal. If the database contains:

```
blue(moon).
blue(biro).
```

then:

```
?- blue(X),write(X),nl,fail.
moon
biro
no
```

functor(T,F,N)

When T is instantiated to a structure, then invoking this predicate will cause F to be matched with the functor of the structure and N to be matched with its arity. For example:

```
?- functor(choice(lager,scotch,vodka),F,N).
F = choice
N = 3
yes
```

If T is not instantiated then both F and N must be. T will then become a structure with functor F and N arguments, each of which will be an uninstantiated variable. For example:

```
?- functor(T,griller,2).
T = griller(_100102,_100103)
yes
```

get(X)

This instantiates X to the next printable character typed – its ASCII code must be 32 <= X <= 255. The character typed must be followed by <Enter>. For example:

```
?- get(X),nl.
^H /* User types 'backspace' - get ignores... */
p /* ...user types 'p'... */
X = 112 /* ...X instantiated to ASCII code for 'p' */
```

get0(X)

This instantiates X to the next character typed irrespective of what that character may be. The character typed will be read immediately by **get0**, i.e. it need not by followed by <Enter>. For example:

```
?- get0(X),nl.
^H /* User types backspace... */
X = 8 /* ...X instantiated to ascii code for BS */
```

halt

This exits the Prolog system and returns the user to the operating system. It closes all files and the contents of the internal database will be lost.

helpfile

This results in the on-line help file being displayed on the screen a "page" at a time. On the Archimedes, the end of each page a message is displayed at the bottom of the screen thus:

More?

Pressing any key other than <Ctrl c> will display the next page from the help file. Pressing <Ctrl c> will display the message line (on the PC only):

Help(h) Quit K-Prolog(q) Abort Query(y/n)

Pressing **h** will display a smaller help screen detailing some of the common predicates you will need. Pressing **q** will quit the interpreter. Pressing **y** will stop displaying the help file, and pressing **n** will continue with its display.

Archimedes users may well prefer to have the help file (**help_pro**) permanently displayed in the editor, allowing them to scroll through it at will.

On the PC the help file is displayed using the supplied "show" program, which allows the user to use the cursor keys to navigate the file. File **show.exe** must be in Prolog's home directory.

integer(X)

The goal **integer(X)** will succeed if X currently stands for an integer. For example, given the facts:

```
year(academic).
year(1991).
```

then:

```
?- year(X).
X = academic
```

```
yes
?- year(X),integer(X).
X = 1991
yes
```

X is Y

Y must be instantiated to an expression composed of numbers, arithmetic operators and variables which, at the time of evaluation, must be instantiated to numbers or other arithmetic expressions. X must be uninstantiated or instantiated to the value of the arithmetic expression Y. The arithmetic expression will then be evaluated and its value (result) will be matched with X. Arithmetical operators that are supported are + (addition), − (subtraction), / (real division), // (integer division), * (multiplication) and the remainder function mod (all infix). For example, given the following Prolog:

```
pop(china,800).
area(china,4).
density(X,Y):-
    pop(X,P),
    area(X,A),
    Y is P/A.
```

then:

```
?- density(china,X).
X = 200
yes
```

In order to obtain a real result, at least one of the arguments to the real division operator / must be real, for example:

```
?- X is 5/2. /* both arguments to / are integers...*/
X = 2 /* ...so X is integer */
yes
?- X is 5/2.0. /* RHS of / is real... */
X = 2.5 /* ...so X is real */
yes
```

Note that because the left-hand side of **is** must be uninstantiated or the value of the expression, there is no "destructive" assignment in Prolog. The following goal would therefore fail:

```
?- X is 5, write(X), nl, X is 6, write(X), nl.
5
no
```

Finally, here is an example that illustrates the difference between = and **is**:

```
?- X = 5 - 2, Y is X.
X = 5 - 2
Y = 3
yes
```

Here X has become matched with the *expression* **5 - 2**, through the use of **=**, while Y has become instantiated to the result of the *evaluation* of the expression **5 - 2**, through the use of `is`.

listing

With no parameter this will list the contents of the internal database to the screen. With a single parameter that corresponds to a functor, it will list all the clauses with that functor (regardless of arity) to the screen.

log(F) (PC only)

This starts logging the Prolog session to file name **F**. It always opens a new file, so it cannot be used to append to an existing log file. If logging fails to write to the file (because the disk is full or any other reason) logging is turned off, an error message is output and an attempt is made to close the log file. Any msaved programs will not be able to use log; you should recreate the msaved files using consult and msave. Logging can be turned off with close_log.

menu_entry(X,Y) (Archimedes only)

This creates an entry on a user-defined menu that can be accessed from the main Prolog menu. **x** is an atom that will be the label for the menu entry, **Y** is an atom that will be the goal executed when the menu entry **x** is selected. See Appendix C for further information and examples.

menu_heading(X) (Archimedes only)

This creates an entry on the main Prolog menu for a user-defined pull-right menu. The atom **x** will be the label for the entry on the main menu. See Appendix C for further information and examples.

messages(X)

This can be used to change and interrogate the status of system message output. The default setting is off, resulting in messages from the Prolog system (e.g. those for garbage collection, the automatic reclamation of memory that is no longer in use) not being output to the screen. Examples are:

```
?- messages(on).
yes
?- messages(off).
yes
?- messages(X).
X = off
yes
```

mload(F)

This loads the msaved file represented by **F**. A Prolog program can be saved using **msave** in an "image format" for very fast loading using the **mload** predicate. Within any session of Prolog, **mload** must be the very first goal executed. If there is a rule with the head **autoexec** (no parameters) in the msaved file, this will be automatically executed. See below for details of using **msave**.

msave(F)

This will save the current contents of the internal database, to the file represented by **F**, in an image format that will facilitate extremely fast loading. This is intended for use with very large Prolog programs. For example, to create a fast-loading version of the Open University **MIKE** system:

```
?- consult('mike.pl').
yes
```

This may take 1 or 2 minutes on less powerful machines. When consulted, save it using msave:

```
?- msave(qmike).
yes
```

This creates a mload-able file called **qmike**, which can be loaded in seconds using **?- mload(qmike).** If the file does not exist it will be created; if it already exists its contents will be overwritten.

name(A,L)

This predicate relates an atom to the list of characters (ASCII codes) that make it up, and can be used either to find the characters for a given atom or to find the atom that has some given characters. For example:

```
?- name(apple,X).
X = [97,112,112,108,101]
yes
```

```
?- name(X,[97,112,112,108,101]).
X = apple
yes
```

nl

This forces subsequent output to begin on a new line. For example:

```
?- assert(blue(moon)).
yes
?- assert(blue(biro)).
yes
?- blue(X),write(X),fail.
moonbirono
?- blue(X),write(X),nl,fail.
moon
biro
no
```

nonvar(X)

The goal **nonvar(X)** will succeed if X is not currently an uninstantiated variable, and is therefore the opposite of **var(X)**. For example, given the fact:

```
blue(moon).
```

then:

```
?- nonvar(X).
no
?- blue(X),nonvar(X).
yes
```

nospy(X)

This removes the spy point on the goal indicated by the functor **x**. For example:

```
?- nospy(append).
```

removes the spy point from **append** (if there is one).

nospyall

This removes all spy points.

not(X)

If X is instantiated to a term that can be interpreted as a goal, then the goal **not(X)** will succeed if an attempt to satisfy the goal X fails, and vice versa. For example, given the fact:

```
blue(moon).
```

then:

```
?- not(blue(X)).
no
```

notrace

This turns off debugging, which is turned on by **trace** (see below).

op(P,Pattern,Symbol)

This predicate allows you to define new Prolog operators, which are either infix (coming between their arguments) or prefix (coming before their argument). It is necessary to specify the operator's precedence and associativity. The precedence determines the order of evaluation when used in a situation that would otherwise be ambiguous. For example, when the expression **a+b*c** is evaluated, the multiplication is done before the addition because the plus is declared internally in the Prolog system to have a higher precedence than multiplication. It is also necessary to specify the associativity. This is required when the same operator (functor) is used more than once in an expression without brackets. In the case of infix operators it specifies whether the expression to the left of the operator should be evaluated before or after the expression on the right. This information is supplied by providing a pattern for the operator, taking one of the following forms:

```
fx, fy, xfx, xfy, yfx, yfy
```

The **y** indicates the expression to be evaluated first and the **x** indicates the evaluation of the expression is to be "delayed". For example:

```
?- op(40,fx,with).
yes
?- assert(with tom).
yes
?- with X.
X = tom
yes
?- op(60,xfy,and).
yes
?- assert(beer and skittles).
```

171

```
yes
?- X and Y.
X = beer
Y = skittles
yes
```

Note that despite the use of the word "operator", no operations on data are defined or performed when the new operators are defined or invoked. They simply bind arguments together in some way similar to that of functors.

put(X)

This writes the character represented by the ASCII code X to the standard output (the screen, unless output has been redirected using **tell**). For example:

```
?- put(104), put(101), put(108), put(108), put(111),
put(10).
hello
yes
```

rand(X)

This instantiates X to a new random number. X on the PC is in the range 0–32,767. X on the Archimedes X is in the range 1 to 7fffffffff.

read(X)

This reads the next term from the current input (the keyboard, unless redirected by **see**) and matches it to its argument X. Note that read can only have one argument. The term must be terminated with a full-stop and carriage return. For example:

```
?- read(X).
date( 1, october, 91). /* typed in by user */
X = date(1,october,91)
```

real(X)

This succeeds when its argument is instantiated to a real number. For example:

```
?- X is 22/7, real(X).
no
?- X is 22.0/7, real(X).
```

```
X = 3.14286
yes
```

reconsult(F)

This reads the Prolog clauses in file **F** into the database. Any clauses already in the database with the same functor and arity as any in the file reconsulted will be replaced by those in the file. All clauses forming a single rule should be contiguous in a file; if they are not then Keylink Prolog will issue a warning: **Clauses not together in rule: predname/arity**. **reconsult** is therefore the same as consult.

reinitialise

This reinitializes the interpreter. The internal database is cleared. The current proof is abandoned and any **prolog.ini** (PC) or **prolog_ini** (Archimedes) file is consulted.

repeat

The **repeat** predicate gives us a way of generating multiple solutions through backtracking which can be used with goals that would otherwise succeed only once (they cannot be resatisfied), e.g. **get**, **get0**, **read**, etc. The following example could have been used to define **get(X)** in terms of **repeat** and **get0(X)** – it will go on reading characters until it finds a printable character (ASCII code >= 32). Note that an attempt to implement this code would result in the message **ERROR - illegal functor** as **get(X)** is already defined as a built-in predicate. For example:

```
get(X):-
    repeat,
    get0(X),
    X >= 32,!.
```

retract(X)

If X can be matched with a fact in Prolog's database, that fact will be removed from the database and cannot be reinstated even if backtracking occurs. For example:

```
?- listing.
blue(moon). /* Database has two 'blue(X)' clauses */
blue(biro).
yes
?- retract(blue(X)).
```

173

```
X = moon; /* User types ';'... */
X = biro; /* ...user types ';' again... */
no /* ...no more clauses matching
blue(X) */
?- listing. /* Database is now empty */
yes
```

save(X)

This writes (saves) the contents of Prolog's database to the file represented by "X", which must be either an appropriately instantiated variable, an atom or a string. If the file exists on disk before **save** is invoked, its contents will be destroyed. This predicate is of very limited use unless you make extensive use of **?- consult(user)** to enter clauses to the database. It is always preferable to work with an editor to create a file that you then consult, and to make any modifications to the file using the editor. For example:

```
?- save('work.pl'). /* save database to 'work.pl' */
```

see(F)

This directs standard input to the file represented by **F**, which must be an atom, a quoted string or a variable instantiated to one of these. This allows Prolog to receive input from any ordinary text file. All input predicates (i.e. **read, get, get0**) take their input from the specified file. Input is redirected to the keyboard by using the predicate **?- seen.** For example, assuming the file **data** contains the following:

```
george.
peter.
```

then the goal:

```
?- see(data),read(X),read(Y),seen.
```

opens the file data for standard input, reads both lines via **read(X)**, **read(Y)** and closes the file. It produces:

```
X = george
Y = peter
```

seed(X)

This uses X as a seed for a new random number sequence.

seeing(X)

This succeeds if input is currently directed, via **see(X)**, to the file **x**. If X is an uninstantiated variable it will be instantiated to the name of the **see** file, otherwise it must represent the name of the file. For example:

```
?- see('input.pro'),seeing(X),seen.
X = input.pro
yes
```

seen

This causes input to be redirected from a file to the keyboard. It can also be used after **consult(user)** to regain the query prompt. For example:

```
?- consult(user). /* Switch to 'input mode'... */
|: bike(yamaha,rd350). /* goes direct to database */
?- seen. /* return to 'query mode' */
yes
?- listing.
bike(yamaha,rd350)
yes
```

Note that the **?-** must be typed before the **seen** predicate and that when it is obeyed by the Prolog system the **?-** prompt appears. This is a quick and easy way to enter clauses into the database, but you will almost certainly find it more convenient to use an editor to create and amend files of your Prolog clauses and to consult those files.

shell (PC only)

This interrupts the Prolog session and returns the user to the operating system. To return to Prolog, the user should type **exit**, and a reminder of this is displayed on the screen above the usual DOS prompt. While execution of Prolog is interrupted the user may perform other tasks, but should note that Prolog is still resident in memory, and that because of this there may not be sufficient memory left to run some other tasks. For example:

```
?- shell. /* takes user out of Prolog to DOS */
Microsoft(R) MS-DOS(R) Version 3.21
    (C)Copyright Microsoft Corp 1981-1987
To return to Prolog, type 'exit'
C:\PROLOG> print animal.pro /* user prints a file... */
C:\PROLOG>ANIMAL.PRO is currently being printed
To return to Prolog, type 'exit'
C:\PROLOG>exit /* ...and returns to Prolog session */
?-
```

175

show_file(X,N)

This writes the contents of a file to the current output. Its main purpose is to display the contents of text files to the screen. The argument N represents the number of lines from the file that will be displayed at a time. For example:

```
?- show_file(temp,20).
```

writes the contents of file **temp** to the current output 20 lines at a time. After each N lines are displayed, the message **More?** is issued. You should respond to this as detailed under **helpfile** above. It is particularly useful on the Archimedes when used in conjunction with the **system** command.

spy(X)

This places a spy point on rule with functor **x**. It causes tracing to start at the point of executing the given rule. For example:

```
?- spy(append).
```

places a spy point on **append**. Tracing will start the first time **append** is called.

stats, statsd

These predicates are provided to give information about the use of memory (expressed as a percentage of the total available) within the interpreter and other information about the current Prolog session. The output from **stats** will look like:

```
Attempted unifications: 346
Constants..23%
```

The output from statsd looks like:

```
Goals..10%..Frames..12%..Varheap..15%..Trail..16%..Backstack..4%
```

Note that the output from **statsd** appears on a single line. This means that, while monitoring the consumption of memory during program execution, the difference between the various figures as indicated by successive calls to **statsd** can be easily seen, as they will "line up" on the screen.

system(X)

This allows the execution of an operating system command from within Prolog. For example (on the PC):

```
?- system('dir animal.pl').
```

executes the DOS command **dir animal.pl**, and writes:

```
Volume in drive C is ROBS_PC
Volume Serial Number is 1C65-035F
Directory of C:\PROLOG
ANIMAL PL 102 31-10-90 14:37
1 File(s) 102 bytes
1255424 bytes free
yes
?-
```

Note for Archimedes users about **system**

No screen output will occur when calling **system(X)** on the Archimedes. Possible applications of **system(X)** include changing the current directory, changing environment variables and creating or changing files. For example, you could redirect output of a "cat" into a file, then display the file. It might be convenient to define this as a rule and store it in the **prolog_ini** file so that it is always available. For example:

```
cat:-
    system('cat { > $.tempcat }'),
    show_file('$.tempcat',10).
```

where **show_file(X)** is the built-in predicate that displays the contents of a given file, a given number of lines at a time. Other possible uses of **system(X)** are considered in the Appendix C, and see also **wimp_task**.

---

tab(X)

This writes X number of spaces to the output. For example:

```
?- tab(10),write(hello),nl.
         hello
yes
```

tell(X)

This causes output to go to file **x** instead of to the screen. Its argument may be a string, an atom or an instantiated variable. Only one **tell** file can be open at any time; if the named file does not exist it will be created, otherwise it will be overwritten. For example:

```
?- listing.
blue(moon).
yes
```

```
?- tell(tellfile).
yes
?- blue(X),write(X),told.
X = moon
yes
```

File **tellfile** will now contain

```
moon
```

telling(X)

This succeeds if output is currently directed to file X through the use of tell(X), and, where X is an uninstantiated variable, unifies its parameter with the name of the file. For example:

```
?- tell('output.pro'),telling(X),told.
X = output.pro
```

told

This closes the current output file, opened via **tell(X)**, and redirects standard output to the screen. Note that if **tell(X)** is reinvoked with the same file name as used before, its former contents will be lost.

trace

This turns on debugging. A step-by-step account of the Prolog execution is sent to the screen. After each line of trace output the user can press <Enter> to obtain the next line of trace. This is known as stepping through the execution. You can also respond with <s>, which will skip the tracing of the current goal, or <n>, which will terminate tracing. On the Windows and Archimedes versions the same effect is achieved by responding to "buttons". This is described in the Appendices B and C respectively.

true

This a goal that always succeeds and that may be used to force Prolog to attempt to satisfy subsequent subgoals even if an earlier goal has failed. For example:

```
?- 5 < 3, write(yes), nl.
no
?- (5 < 3 ; true), write(yes), nl.
yes
yes
```

var(X)

This succeeds if its argument is currently an uninstantiated variable. For example, given the fact:

```
blue(danube).
then:
?- blue(X),var(X).
no
```

wimp_task(A) (Archimedes only)

This starts a new WIMP task. Its argument is the CLI command necessary to run the task. For example, if **regions** is a text file, then:

```
?- wimp_task(regions).
```

will cause the file regions to be edited: the editor will be invoked and will read in the regions file.

write(X)

This causes its argument to be written to the current output. It can take only one argument. For example, given the fact:

```
fish(scales,fins).
```

then:

```
?- fish(X,Y),write('fish have '),write(X),
write(' and '),write(Y),nl.
fish have scales and fins
X = scales
Y = fins
yes
```

Archimedes only

The following predicates have been provided for making SWI (software interrupt) calls, and for allocating, setting and freeing memory.

os_free(B)

This frees memory allocated (**via os_malloc**) at address **B**.

os_getbyte(B,Offset,Val)

This returns the value **Val** of a byte at address **B + Offset**.

os_malloc(B,Size)

This allocates a block of **Size** bytes of memory (zeroed), and returns the address in **B**. **B** has internal type "address" and cannot be used in arithmetic.

os_putbyte(B,Offset,Val)

This puts a single byte, value **Val**, at **address B + Offset**.

os_putint(B,Offset,Val)

This puts an integer, value **Val**, at address **B + Offset**.

os_putstring(B,Offset,Val)

This puts a string **Val** at address **B + Offset**. **Val** should be an atom. The string will be terminated in memory with a zero byte.

os_reg(Rno,Val)

This returns the value **Val** of register **Rno** as set by the last SWI made.

os_swi(SWInum,Reg)

This calls software interrupt **SWInum** with registers having the values given by the list in **Reg**. The interrupt number can be either an integer or a hex number given in single quotes (an atom).

Here are some examples:

```
/* make a call to OS_SWINumberToString to get the name of
SWI 56: produces 'OS_SWINumberToString' */
test1:-
    os_malloc(B,40),
    os_swi(56,[56,B,40]),
    os_reg(2,Len),
    out_string(B,Len),
    nl.
out_string(B,L):-
    Len is L - 1,
    out_string1(B,0,Len).
out_string1(B,N,L):-
    N < L,
```

```
        !,
        os_getbyte(B,N,X),
        put(X),
        M is N + 1,
        out_string1(B,M,L).
    out_string1(_,_,_).
```

The following predicate **wimp_error** displays the standard error box on the screen given a program name and some message.

```
    wimp_error(Progname,Message):- /* takes 2 atoms */
        os_malloc(B,80),
        os_putint(B,0,0),
        os_putstring(B,4,Message),
        os_swi('400df',[B,0,Progname]),
        os_free(B).
```

APPENDIX A
Installing Prolog

A.1 Installing Keylink Prolog on a PC (DOS)

Keylink Prolog may be executed directly from the floppy disk by typing **prolog**. Alternatively, it may be installed on a hard disk. The following assumes you are installing on a hard disk drive, designated **c:**. From the root directory create a directory called **KPROLOG** with **md kprolog**. Change to this directory with **cd kprolog**. Copy the entire contents of the Keylink Prolog distribution disk to the current directory with **copy a:*.***. (You may need to substitute **b:** for **a:** if you are using floppy drive b:.) You may now run Keylink Prolog by typing **prolog**. If you wish to run Keylink Prolog from any directory then add **;c:\kprolog** to the "path" statement in your **autoexec.bat** file. You should be aware, however, of the implications this may have on the reading of the **prolog.ini** file (see below for details of this). See your DOS manual for details of the **PATH** command (defining a search path).

A.2 Installing Keylink Prolog on a PC (Windows 3.1)

You should copy all the supplied files into a directory called **KPROLOG** as for MS DOS.
1. From within Windows, invoke the Program Manager.
2. Select **New** from the **File** menu by clicking on the **File** menu and then **New**.
3. Select **Program item OK**.
4. Fill in the description as Keylink Prolog.
5. Click on **Browse** and use the file selector to select the **KPROLOG** directory.
6. Select the **wprolog.exe** task and then click on **OK**.

7. Make the same directory, or any other you choose, the working directory.

If you have any problems with the above, see the Microsoft Windows *User's Guide*. Double clicking on the Keylink Prolog icon **?-** will start Keylink Windows Prolog.

A.3 Installing Keylink Prolog on a RM Nimbus file server

The program files need to be copied onto the file server disk and placed in the public drive. This entails the following sequence:

- Log on as system manager.
- Place the distribution disk in an available drive.
- Select the M drive with:

  M:<CR>

- Change to the **M:** **PUBLIC** subdirectory using:

  CD M:\PUBLIC<CR>

- Make a directory to store the program and its associated files using the command:

  MD KPROLOG<CR>

- Change to the new directory with:

  CD KPROLOG<CR>

- Use the following commands to copy the Prolog files into the new application directory:

  COPY A:\PROLOG.EXE M:<CR>

  COPY A:\INIT.DAT M:<CR>

- Ensure that these files have the "read only" attribute to prevent access violation error messages when multiple access takes place by using the command:

  ATTRIB +R *.*<CR>

- Return to the **M:\PUBLIC** directory by typing:

  CD ..<CR>

- Create a file called **i.iKPROLOG.BAT;** containing the command:

  P:\KPROLOG\PROLOG<CR>

- Make **KPROLOG.BAT** "read only" using:

  ATTRIB +R KPROLOG.BAT<CR>

- Network users will now be able to run Prolog by typing the command:

  KPROLOG <CR>

A.4 Installing Prolog on an Archimedes

Before running or installing Prolog make a copy of the Keylink Prolog floppy disk and use the copy. (Keep the original somewhere safe, just in case the copy gets corrupted.) Where reference is made to the Keylink Prolog floppy disk, use the copy.

A.4.1 Running Prolog from a floppy disk

The Keylink Prolog floppy disk contains an applications directory called !Kprolog. This contains all of Keylink Prolog. However, Kprolog uses some of the "modules" that exist in the !system directory of Archimedes systems. The necessary system files are included on the Keylink disk for convenience in a minimal system folder. This means that you can run Kprolog directly from the distribution disk.

If you have two floppy disk drives you could have your own system disk in one drive and the Kprolog disk in the other.

To run Kprolog double click on the !Kprolog icon.

A.4.2 Installing Prolog on a hard disk

The following assumes that your hard disk is designated 4 and your floppy drive is designated 0.

Open the directory windows for the hard disk and the Prolog floppy disk (this is done by double clicking the bar icons 4 and 0). Create and open a subdirectory on the hard disk for the new Kprolog application (if you have an existing applications directory then open it if you do not want to create a new one for Kprolog). From the Keylink floppy disk window pick up the !Kprolog icon (by positioning the pointer and pressing the left mouse button) and drag the icon into the hard disk application directory window (by moving the mouse while keeping the left mouse button pressed). Now release the icon (stop pressing the left mouse button).

There should now be a new directory icon in the hard disk window called !Kprolog. You should make sure that your own system folder contains modules of the same or later version number than those in the minimal system folder supplied.

A.4.3 Installing on an Acorn network file server

The installation procedure is the same as for a hard disk given above except that you must ensure that read/write attributes are set to allow general read but not write permissions. The Prolog system files should be stored in a suitable public area on the network, although users will save and load program files from their own space. It is recommended that each

Prolog user should have a separate directory for Prolog files in their own space.

Prolog is now installed, but before doing anything else remove the Keylink Prolog floppy disk from its drive, and switch off your Archimedes for about 30 seconds. Kprolog will be ready to use when you next switch your computer on.

To run Kprolog double click on the **!Kprolog** icon.

A.5 Initialization file

Whenever Keylink Prolog is started it looks in the current directory for a file called **prolog.ini** on the PC and **prolog_ini** on the Archimedes. If it finds such a file it attempts to consult (read) it and load it into the Prolog database. If there is no such file it proceeds without loading anything. Frequently used rules and/or facts may therefore usefully be placed in such a file, and will then be accessible to the user each time Keylink Prolog is started. An example that uses this file to define permanently an edit predicate for the PC DOS version is given in the next section.

If you are using a PC, and have modified the path statement in the file **autoexec.bat** to enable running Keylink Prolog from any directory, the file **prolog.ini** will not be found and consulted unless it exists in the directory from which you are running Prolog. This problem can be resolved by adding the line **append c:\kprolog** to your **autoexec.bat** file, or by adding **;c:\kprolog** to an existing **append** statement. This assumes that Keylink Prolog resides in directory **kprolog** on hard drive **c:**.

A.6 Using Prolog with an editor under DOS

The following piece of Prolog defines a predicate edit that enables a file to be edited from Keylink Prolog using an editor of the user's choice (in the example this is called **vi**). This rule is explained more fully in Chapter 5 but is included here because of its immediate usefulness. This code can usefully be placed in the **prolog.ini** file in the directory from which you run Prolog so that the edit facility so defined is always available (or use an **append** statement as detailed above).

```
edit(File):-
    name(File,Flist),
    append("vi ",Flist,L),
    name(S,L),
    system(S),
    reconsult(File).
append([],L,L).
```

186

```
append([H|T],L,[H|U]):-
    append(T,L,U).
```

You should replace **vi** with the editor of your choice. This code is discussed more fully in section 5.5, Editing on the PC.

A.7 Using Prolog with an editor under Windows

You can use any editor of your choice. Notepad is extremely easy to use and is nearly always available. You can start Notepad by double clicking on its icon. Use it to edit your Prolog source file, which you should always arrange to have the file extension **.pl** (Windows Prolog knows to list these files in its file selector). You should always save any changes you make to your Prolog source, but you may leave Notepad running and taking up screen space or you can iconize it. From Prolog the file saved may then be consulted selecting the **File** menu option and then selecting the **Open** menu item. This displays the standard file selector dialogue.

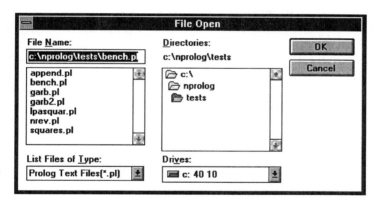

This dialogue allows you to select your recently edited file. The fact that you can leave Notepad running while using Prolog makes it extremely easy to make any further changes that may prove necessary.

A.8 Using Prolog with an editor on an Archimedes

The Archimedes operating system allows several programs to have windows open at the same time. Kprolog runs in a single window and is designed to be used alongside an Archimedes editor (such as !Edit). When developing a Prolog program a second window can be used for editing the program.

After a program has been edited you can load it back into Kprolog using **reconsult**, which overwrites the old rules with the new ones found in the file being reconsulted. Dragging the Kprolog file icon into the Kprolog window has the same effect as reconsulting it, as does selecting **Reconsult** from the **Query** menu.

Prolog for MS Windows

B.1 Introduction

When Windows Prolog is executed it occupies a Window in which the user and program interaction appears and scrolls up the Window much as for the DOS command line version. As for the DOS version, the system starts with the query prompt ?- on the first line after the copyright notice. You can interact immediately with the Prolog system by typing on the keyboard, and the text typed will appear following the ?- prompt.

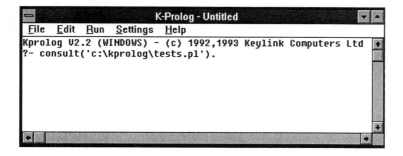

The Window is scrollable by the user via the vertical and horizontal scroll bars at the right and bottom of the window, and text can be retrieved after the point it would normally be lost for a "glass teletype" mode of operation, such as DOS Prolog uses. The Windows version offers many other advantages, such as multitasking, drag and drop file loading, and the common dialogue for file selection. These are discussed in the following sections. For installation see Appendix A.

B.2 Starting Windows Prolog

Double clicking on the Keylink Prolog icon **?-** will start Keylink Windows Prolog. The Prolog window will appear with the query prompt at the top left, and you may start typing your Prolog queries immediately, although you are more likely, in most situations, to want to consult a Prolog source file using one of the Windows-specific features (see §B.6). However, **consult** and **reconsult** can be typed in at the query prompt and will work exactly as normal; the new Windows features simply provide easier ways to effect the same results.

Windows Prolog may be exited by selecting **Exit** from the **File** menu. It can be iconized by selecting the down arrow in the upper-right corner of the window.

B.3 Built-in predicates

Although Windows Prolog has the same functionality as the MS DOS version in most areas, there are a few predicates that make little sense for Windows and which when called will give an error message. These are **shell** and **system**. Because of the multitasking nature of the Windows operating environment, these built-ins are not essential to Windows programming and their functionality can be obtained by direct interaction with the Windows system.

B.4 Multitasking

The major functional difference is that the Windows version is multitasking and frequently yields to the operating system while executing. This is virtually a necessity of any Windows program as it allows other tasks to continue executing. However, it greatly slows the speed of execution even when there are no other tasks currently taking significant processing time. Most importantly for the Keylink Prolog user is that an editor, such as Notepad, can be used at the same time as having Prolog executing. This facilitates rapid program development as it is not necessary to start and stop different applications to complete an edit, compile and run development cycle. Using Prolog with the Notepad editor is described in Appendix A

B.5 Dialogues

There are several situations in which a user response is required before Prolog will continue processing. Typically in the DOS version a single character is typed by the user and the processing continues. Windows always uses a dialogue that specifically prompts a response by requiring the user to click with the mouse on a button. For example, when a query is solved there appears a dialogue that asks the user whether Prolog is to attempt to find a further solution. Also, when tracing Prolog's execution via the **trace** predicate a dialogue is used to determine the user's desired action. The use of these dialogues is convenient as they avoid having to remember specific responses. Examples of these dialogues have been given in the main text.

B.6 Consulting source files

There are several ways in which a Prolog source file may be consulted by Windows Prolog. Prolog source files may be dragged and dropped into the Prolog Window. In order to do this you need to run the Windows File Manager; locate the file that you wish to consult and drag and drop it into the Prolog window using the mouse. You need to hold down the left mouse button while dragging the **File** icon from the File Manager window to the Prolog window. You should consult the Windows User's Guide for instructions if you have difficulties with this operation.

A Prolog source file may also be consulted by selecting **Open** from the **File** menu. This presents you with the common file selector dialogue from which you can select the Prolog source file.

The built-in predicates **consult** and **reconsult** may be used as usual, but you may find it convenient to set the current directory using the **Change directory** menu option of the **File** menu.

B.7 Cutting and pasting

Text from the Prolog window may be cut and copied to the Windows clipboard. Text may also be pasted into the Prolog window from the clipboard. All of these operations can be made using the **Edit** menu options. A particularly useful operation is that of rerunning or editing a previous query by copying it to the clipboard and then pasting it to the query text line.

B.8 Prolog's menus under Windows

Additional functionality that may not have been included in the above may be realized from the following descriptions of all the available menu options.

The main menu headings appear across the top of the window, which can be seen in the illustration of the Prolog window given at the beginning of this appendix.

These have the following submenus which are explained on the right. Where there is an equivalent Prolog built-in predicate, this is given in brackets:

File

New	Clears Prolog's database (**cleardb**)
Open	Consults a file (**reconsult(File)**)
Save	Saves in mload-able format (**msave(File)**)
Save As	Saves in mload-able format (**msave(File)**)
Change directory	Uses file selector to change directory
Exit	Exits Prolog

Edit

Undo	Undoes previous edit in the window
Cut	Deletes and copies to the clipboard
Copy	Copies to the clipboard
Paste	Pastes from the clipboard
Delete	Deletes text from the window

Run

Abort query	Halts the current execution
Pause output	Suspends output
List Prolog clauses	Lists contents of database

Settings

Trace Prolog execution	Turns tracing on/off (trace/notrace)
Messages on	Turns messages on (messages(on/off))

Help

Contents	Help contents
Predicates	Help on built-in predicates
Using help	Help on help
About	Information abut Keylink Prolog

192

Prolog under RiscOS

C.1 About Kprolog

Keylink Prolog takes advantage of the user-friendly window interface of the Archimedes desktop. Kprolog is an application, just like Edit and Paint. Kprolog is stored in an applications directory called !kprolog, and appears as an icon in the form of a red ?- symbol. Kprolog can be started either by double clicking this icon or by double clicking a Kprolog program file (see below). Once Kprolog has been started an icon will be placed on the icon bar (again a red ?- symbol).

We will consider here aspects of Kprolog that have special significance for Archimedes users.

C.2 The icon bar menu

Pressing the middle mouse button when the pointer is over the Kprolog bar icon will cause a menu to appear:

KProlog
Info ->
Quit

There are two choices that can be made. Choosing **Info** (or moving the mouse pointer over the -> arrow) will display information about Kprolog in a window. Clicking the mouse when the pointer is out of this window will close the window.

To finish Kprolog choose **Quit** from this menu. Note that Kprolog can also be quit by entering ?- **halt.** as a query.

C.3 Running Kprolog

Clicking the left mouse button when the pointer is over the bar icon will start Kprolog, and a window will be opened in which queries can be entered.

C.4 The Kprolog window

This is where queries are entered. Pressing the middle mouse button (when the pointer is in the window) displays a menu of functions, each of which is explained below.

KProlog
Trace
Reconsult->
Listing
Messages
Select   ->
Abort query
Clear
Save   ->

When an option is available for selection, it will appear in bold text: unavailable options will appear in fainter text. The **Abort query** option, for example, will be in faint text when the menu is displayed while no query is running.

If tracing is off then **Trace** will appear on the menu as above. If tracing is on then the word **Trace** will be ticked. Selecting **Trace** will toggle the current setting.

Selecting **Reconsult** from the menu displays a dialogue box that contains the name of the most recent file to be consulted (or reconsulted). This option is unavailable until at least one file has been consulted or reconsulted. You can change or overwrite the name of the file in the dialogue box: it will be reconsulted when the **OK** button is selected.

Selecting **Listing** from the menu will display in the Kprolog window all the current facts and rules in the Prolog database.

The **Messages** option can be used to turn off the emission of warning and informational messages. Note that this option can be selected while a file is being consulted. The default is for message emission to be on, and this is indicated by the ✓ against the menu option.

The **Select** option is used to copy selected text to the query line and to cancel the selection of text. Areas of text may be marked (selected) by pressing the left button and dragging the cursor over the required text, which will cause the selected text to be highlighted. The window may be scrolled back in order to locate and select the required text. The text may then be copied to the query line by pressing control-c, or the selection may be cancelled by pressing either control-z or clicking adjust. If the selected text includes a carriage return, the query will nevertheless not be executed until you press carriage return, thus allowing the query line to be edited. Alternatively, the Select option will cause a menu to be displayed.

The selected text can be copied to the query line as described above by selecting the **Copy** option or cancelled by selecting the **Clear** option.

The **Abort query** option will cause the execution of a query that is running to be immediately terminated.

The **Clear** and **Save** options are used to control the text in the Kprolog window

As queries are entered they are scrolled upwards in the window to make room for new ones. The vertical and horizontal scroll bars can be used to view previous queries. Only a certain number of queries can be remembered: when more than this number has been entered the earlier ones are "forgotten". When the output window is nearly full a message to this effect will be displayed, and at this point the log should be saved (see below) if desired. If the output window does become full then, as new information appears, the text at the top of the window will be lost.

The **Clear** menu option causes the entire Kprolog window to be cleared of both the visible part and any queries and output that have scrolled out of view.

The **Save** option allows you to save the entire Kprolog window contents. **Save** will present you with the standard Archimedes window for saving files. Enter the name of the file to which you wish the output log to be written and drag the file icon into a directory. The file will be created if it does not exist; otherwise its existing contents will be appended to, thus allowing a complete log of a Kprolog session to be maintained. Having saved the window contents the window will be cleared.

C.5 Creating a user-defined menu

The built-in predicates **menu_heading(X)** and **menu_entry(X,Y)** are provided, respectively, to allow an additional entry to be attached to the main

Prolog menu, which will display a user-defined menu when selected, and to define the entries on that menu.

The atom **X** in **menu_heading(X)** will label the additional entry in the main menu, and will also be the heading for the user menu. For each entry in the user menu, **menu_entry(X,Y)** should be called, where the atom **X** is the label for the entry and the atom **Y** is the goal to be executed when that entry is selected. Only one level of user menu is supported. The following code defines an additional entry **Tests** on the main Prolog menu, and three entries on the **Tests** menu, **Test a**, **Test b** and **Test c**. Selection of the **Tests** option from the main menu will result in the **Tests** menu being displayed, and selection of an item from that menu will result in one of the goals **a**, **b** or **c** being executed:

```
tests_menu:-
    menu_heading('Tests'),
    menu_entry('Test a', a),
    menu_entry('Test b', b),
    menu_entry('Test c', c).
a:-
    write('goal a executed'), nl.
b:-
    write('goal b executed'), nl.
c:-
    write('goal c executed'), nl.
```

Executing the goal **tests_menu** will add the entry **Tests** to the main menu, which will then look as follows.

Prolog
Trace
Reconsult->
Listing
Select   ->
Abort query
Clear
Save   ->
Tests   ->

Selecting the **Tests** option will cause the **Tests** menu to be displayed.

Tests
Test a
Test b
Test c

196

Selection of one of these items will result in one of the associated goals as defined in **menu_entry** being executed. Note that the goals for the menu entries must be atoms: if a more complicated term is required this should be done using a rule that has the atom as its head and whatever complexity is required as its body. For example, MIKE 2.03 can be given a menu interface by running the following code:

```
setup:-
    menu_heading('mike'),
    menu_entry('Deduce',my_deduce),
    menu_entry('Forward chain - clear wm',fc),
    menu_entry('Forward chain - keep wm',go),
    menu_entry('Show frames',browse),
    menu_entry('Show history',show_history),
    menu_entry('Show rules',show_rules),
    menu_entry('Status',status),
    menu_entry('Show wm',wm),
    menu_entry('Load KB',load_kb).
my_deduce:-
    write('Goal to deduce = '),
    read(X),
    deduce X.
load_kb :-
    write('KB to load = '),
    read(K),
    kb K.
show_history:- show history.
show_rules:- show rules.
```

C.6 Loading programs into Kprolog

There are four ways in which programs can be loaded into Kprolog. The first is by starting Kprolog (by double clicking the **!kprolog** icon) and then entering either a:

```
?- consult(program-name)
```

or a:

```
?- reconsult(program-name)
```

query. A second way is to drag a program icon over the Kprolog bar icon, or into the Kprolog window. Note that Kprolog programs loaded this way must either be text files or special Kprolog files (see the next section).
A third way to load a program into Kprolog only works if the program is a

Kprolog file: simply double clicking on such a file's icon will automatically start Kprolog if it is not running and reconsult the program selected.

Finally, a file may be loaded into Kprolog by selecting **Reconsult** from the main menu of the Kprolog window. See the description of the **Reconsult** option in section 4.

C.7 Files of type Kprolog

Each file on the Archimedes is of a certain type, for example text files, sprite files, directories (a special case), etc. An application such as Edit can automatically be run when a file of its type is double clicked on (e.g. "Text" files). The same is true for files of type "Kprolog" (note that the Archimedes does not mind whether letters are upper or lower case: "text" and "Kprolog" are just as correct). Files created by Edit are of type "Text". However, a file called **myprog** might be a Prolog program that you have written using Edit. When you successfully consult or reconsult **myprog** it will automatically have its type changed to "Kprolog".

You may also change a file's type to Kprolog by using the CLI. Although the CLI is very different from the desktop it can be very useful and not necessarily complicated. An advantage of the desktop is that when you click on a file icon the desktop knows which disk and which directory the file is stored in: when dealing with the CLI you will have to state these.

Let us assume that your disk drive is number 0 (i.e. floppy disk drive – if you are using a hard disk use the number 4). Invoke the CLI by pressing the F12 function key. A white area should appear at the bottom of the screen, and an asterisk (*) prompt will appear. Type:

```
mount 0
    dir adfs::0
```

This tells the CLI to go to the root (top-level) directory for the disk in drive 0. Typing:

```
cat
```

displays a list of files that are on the disk. Let us assume that the file **myprog** is in the directory called **programs**. Move to this directory by typing:

```
dir programs
```

Display the current type of the file **myprog** by typing:

```
info myprog
```

The first word of the of the information displayed is the file name, and the third is the file type. Currently this may be "Text". We can change this to "Kprolog" by typing:

```
settype myprog Kprolog
```

Now **info myprog** displays a file type of "Kprolog". Pressing <Return> at the * prompt in the CLI will take you back to the desktop environment. The icon of file **myprog** will have changed from a text file icon (like a piece of paper with a pencil) to a Kprolog program file icon (like a piece of paper with the **?-** prompt on it). Kprolog can now be started by double clicking on the program file icon.

We will briefly recap the CLI commands we have used above.

- To move to a disk drive (e.g. drive 0) use **dir adfs::0**.
- To change directories (e.g. to directory "programs") use **dir programs**.
- To go to the root directory of the current disk drive use **dir $**.
- To display information about a file (e.g. **myprog**) use **info myprog**.
- To change the type of a file (e.g. change type of **myprog** to "Kprolog") use **settype myprog Kprolog**. To return to the desktop from the CLI press <Return> at the * prompt.

It is useful to know about how the Archimedes refers to where files are in terms of disk drive and directory name. The location of a file expressed in this way is called the path to a file. For example, the path to the file **myprogs** whose file type we have just changed is:

    adfs::0.$.programs.myprogs

Note that the full-stop (.) is used to separate the names of the directories and the file name. A file whose path is :

    adfs::4.$.progs.prolog.append

is the file **append** on disk drive 4 (the hard disk), in the directory **prolog**, which is in the directory **progs**. When using the predicates tell, **msave**, **consult** and **reconsult**, and when saving files from many applications, using the full file path means you know exactly where the file will end up. You can see the paths of directories in the titles of directory windows opened in the desktop. When editing a file in Edit the window title displays the full path of the file.

C.8 Selecting additional solutions

After solving a query, a **Query Action** window will appear. This window contains two buttons (also called *action icons*, like the **OK** button in a **File save** window). These buttons are shown below.

Query Action
Next Solution   Finish Query

Clicking on Next Solution will cause Kprolog to "backtrack" to a choice point, and try to resatisfy the goal with one of the other facts or rules that apply. If the goal succeeds then the alternative solution will be displayed, and the Query Action Window will appear again. This will continue until there are no more choice points or until you click on Finish Query, which causes Kprolog to leave any untried choice points, and wait for the next query to be entered. Note that the Query Action window will only appear if the initial query succeeds and there are untried choices encountered during the satisfaction of the query.

C.9 Tracing a query

Tracing a query also requires interaction with a window. The query `?- trace.` (or choosing **Trace** from the Kprolog window's menu) will put Kprolog into trace mode. In this mode, at each step of a query's solution, information about the current subgoal and variable bindings is displayed in the output window. The following buttons are displayed in a window called **Trace Actions**.

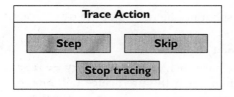

Step tells Kprolog to do the next single action and display information about this action before displaying the **Trace Action** window again. Stepping allows you to see how a query (or part of a query) is solved step by step.

Skip will cause Kprolog to solve the current subgoal, then to display the **Trace Action** window again. However, all the intermediate work of solving the current subgoal is not displayed.

If no more tracing is required then **Stop tracing** should be selected. This will switch off tracing altogether and Kprolog will continue to try to solve the original query without trace output.

The trace options are used when debugging (correcting) Prolog programs, or when trying to understand what a rule or collection of rules is actually doing.

C.10 The `system` built-in predicate

The **system** predicate allows you to execute CLI commands from within Kprolog. No text output will result from a system query, but it can change CLI variables and start other programs running. For example, when using the CLI there is the concept of "current directory", e.g.

```
dir adfs::4.$.programs
```

tells the CLI to make the **programs** directory on the hard disk (drive 4) the current directory. The Kprolog query:

```
?- system('dir adfs::4.$.programs').
```

has the same effect on the CLI current directory. Now a **consult** query such as:

```
?- consult(myprog).
```

will result in Kprolog looking for the program **myprog** in the current CLI directory (which has been set to **programs**). The same effect could be achieved by including the complete path of a file in the **consult** query:

```
?- consult('adfs::4.$.programs.myprog').
```

but this involves more typing, i.e. the complete path needs to be given for every **consult** or **reconsult**. By setting the current directory using **system** and **dir**, and having related programs in the same directory, several simpler consults can be used. This has the added advantage that, if the program directory is moved, only the **system** query will need to be changed. When writing large prolog programs it is useful to have a rule that automatically consults or reconsults the other program files, for example:

```
load_files:-
    system('dir adfs::4.$.programs'),
    consult(rules1),
    consult(rules2),
    consult(data).
```

Here is a short rule to change the file type of a given file to "Kprolog":

```
make_kprolog(Filename):-
    /* assume file is in current directory */
    name('settype ',Set_chars),
    name(Filename,File_chars),
    name(' Kprolog',Kprolog_chars),
    append(Set_chars,File_chars,Temp_chars),
    append(Temp_chars,Kprolog_chars,CLI_chars),
    name(CLI_command,CLI_chars),
    system(CLI_command).
```

Note that this rule assumes that **append** is defined. It uses the **name** built-in predicate to create a single list of characters that takes the form

settype <file> Kprolog, where **<file>** is the file name. This list of characters is then converted back into an atom and given as a parameter to the **system** built-in predicate.

References

Ait-Kaci, H. 1991. *Warren's abstract machine – a tutorial reconstruction*. Cambridge, Mass.: MIT Press.

Boolos, G. S. & R. C. Jeffrey 1974. *Computability and logic*. Cambridge: Cambridge University Press.

Buchanan, B. G. & E. H. Shortliffe 1984. *Rule based expert systems*. Reading, Mass.: Addison Wesley.

Chang, C. & R. Lee 1973. *Symbolic logic and mechanical theorem proving*. New York: Academic Press.

Clocksin, W. F. & C. S. Mellish 1981. *Programming in Prolog*. New York: Springer.

Colmerauer, A. 1973. *Etude et realisation d'un systeme PROLOG*. Convention de Research IRIA – Sesori No. 77030.

Dobry, T. P. 1990. *A high performance architecture for Prolog*. Norwell, Mass.: Kluwer Academic Publishers.

Dodd, T. 1990. *Prolog – a logical approach*. Oxford: Oxford University Press.

Dowsing, R. D. 1986. *A first course in formal logic and its applications in computer science*. Oxford: Blackwell Scientific Publications.

Duda, R., J. Gaschnig, P. Hart 1979. Model design in the prospector consultant system for mineral exploration. In *Expert systems in the micro electronic age*, D. Michie (ed.), 153–67. Edinburgh: Edinburgh University Press.

Feigenbaum, E. A. 1979. Themes and case studies of knowledge engineering. In *Expert systems in the micro electronic age*, D. Michie (ed.), 3–25. Edinburgh: Edinburgh University Press.

Gray, P. 1984. *Logic, algebra and databases*. Chichester: Ellis Horwood.

O'Keefe, R. A. 1990. *The craft of Prolog*. Cambridge, Mass.: MIT Press.

Kogge, P. M. 1991. *The architecture of symbolic computers*. New York: McGraw-Hill.

Lindsay, R. K., B.G. Buchanan, E. A. Feigenbaum 1980. *Applications of artificial intelligence in organic chemistry*. McGraw-Hill.

Lucas, R. J. 1988. *Database applications using Prolog*. Chichester: Ellis Horwood.

Maier, D. & D. S. Warren 1988. *Computing with logic – logic programming with Prolog*. Benjamin Cummings Publishing.

Rayward-Smith, V. J. 1983. *A first course in formal language theory*. Oxford: Blackwell Scientific Publications.

Robinson, J. A. J. 1965. A machine orientated logic based on the resolution principle. *Journal of the Association of Computing Machinery* **12**, 23–41.

Sterling, L. & E. Shapiro 1986. *The art of Prolog advanced programming techniques.* Cambridge, Mass.: MIT Press.

Warren, D. & F. Pereira 1981. *An efficient easily adaptable system for interpreting natural language queries.* Report No. 155, February 1981. Department of Artificial Intelligence, University of Edinburgh.

Solutions to selected exercises

Exercises 1a

2.
- (a) if
- (b)   database
- (c) instantiated
- (d) backtracking
- (e) unification
- (f) built-in predicates

Exercises 1b

3.
(a)

```
?- car(ford, Mod, Trim, Country, Cc, Type, Price),
   write(Mod),nl,
   write(Trim),nl,
   write(Country),nl,
   write(Cc),nl,
   write(Type),nl,
   write(Price),nl,
   fail.
```

(b)

```
?- car(ford, Mod, Trim, Country, Cc, Type, Price),
   Cc > 1300,
   Price < 9000.
```

(c)

```
?- car(rover, ModRover, _, _, _, _, PriceRover),
   car(fiat, ModFiat, _, _, _, _, PriceFiat),
   PriceRover > PriceFiat,
   write(ModRover),nl,
   fail.
```

Exercises 1c

2.

```
?- car(Man, metro, mg, Country, _, _, _),
   supplier(Man,Country,Address,_).
```

3.

```
?- car(Man, _, _, uk, _, saloon, _),
   supplier(Man,uk,_,Tel).
```

4.

```
?- car(Man, _, _, _, Cc, _, _),
   Cc > 1300,
   supplier(Man,_,_,Tel).
```

Exercises 2

1. head, body

4.

```
happened_before(Event1, Event2):-
    event(Event1, T1),
    event(Event2, T2),
    T1 < T2.
```

6.

```
car_body_points(estate, 1).
    car_body_points(saloon, 2).
    .
    .
    .
```

7.

```
total_points(Man, Mod, Total):-
```

```
        car(Man, Mod, _, _, Cc, Type, _),
        risk_for_capacity(Cc, Cpoints),
        car_hbody_points(Type, Bpoints),
        Total is Cpoints + Bpoints.
```

Exercises 3

1.

```
    father(harold,charles).
    mother(harold,diana).
    father(charles,philip).
    mother(charles,elizabeth).
    father(philip.john).
    father(philip,mary).
    father(elizabeth,edward).
    mother(elizabeth,helen).
    ancestor(A, B):-
        parent(A, B).
    ancestor(A, B):-
        parent(A, C),
        ancestor(C, B).
    parent(A, B):-
        father(A, B).
    parent(A, B):-
        mother(A, B).
```

3.

```
    mod5(X, Y):-
        X >= 5,
        X1 is X - 5,
        mod5(X1, Y).
    mod5(X, X):-
        X >= 0,
        X < 5.
```

4.

```
    power(X, 0, 1).
        power(X, N, P):-
        N > 0,
        N1 is N - 1,
        power(X, N1, P1),
```

```
P is X * P1.
```

Exercises 4

1.

```
push(X):-
        asserta(stack(X)).
   pop(X):-
        retract(stack(X)).
```

2.

```
stack_size(N):-
     count(stack(X),N).
```

3.

```
stack_clear:-
     abolish(stack,1).
```

Exercises 5a

1.
- (a) 1
- (b) 2
- (c) 2

2.
- (a) X = frame
     Y = wheels(spokes,hub)
     Z = handlebar
- (b) X = preface
     Y = contents
     Z = section(paragraph)

Exercises 5b

1. Principal functor = sentence with components: **noun_phrase** (adjective,noun) and **verb_phrase**. Its first component has functor **noun_phrase** with components adjective and noun.

3.

```
postorder(Name):-
     management_tree(X,Name,manages(N1,N2)),
```

```
      postorder(N1),
      postorder(N2),
      write(Name),nl.
```

4.

```
   preorder(Name):-
      preorder(Name,0).
   preorder(null,_).
   preorder(Name,N):-
      management_tree(X,Name,manages(N1,N2)),
      tab(N),
      write(Name),nl,
      M is N + 4,
      preorder(N1,M),
      preorder(N2,M).
```

Exercises 6

1.

```
   weekdays([monday,tuesday,wednesday,thursday,⌐
   friday,saturday,sunday]).
```

2.

```
   day(Date, Day):-
      Date <= 7,
      weekdays(W),
      getnth(Date, W, Day).
   day(Date, Day):-
      Day > 7,
      Date1 is Date - 7,
      day(Date1, Day).
```

3.

```
   delete(X, [X, [X|L1], L1).
      delete(X, [H|L1], [H|L2]):-
         delete(X, L1, L2).
```

4.

```
   last_element([X], X).

      last_element([_|T], X):-
         last_element(T, X).
```

5.

```
intersect([], _, []).
intersect([H|T], L, [H|R]):-
    member(H, L),
    intersect(T, L, R).
intersect([_|T], L, R):-
    intersect(T, L, R).
```

6.

```
union([], L, L).
    union([H|T], L, R):-
    member(H, L),
    !,
    union(T, L, R).
union([H|T], L, [H|R]):-
    union(T, L, R).
```

7.

```
reverse([], []).
reverse([H|T], Reversed):-
    reverse(T, R),
    append(R, [H], Reversed).
```

Exercises 7

1.

```
correct_word(W):-
    word(W).
near_miss(Word, NearWord):-
    word(NearWord),
    name(Word, Lword),
    name(NearWord, LNearWord),
    length(Word, LenWord),
    length(NearWord, LenNearWord),
    close_numbers(LenWord, LenNearWord),
    first_three_equal(LWord, LNearWord).
first_three_equal([H1,H2,H3|__], [H1,H2,H3|_]).
close_numbers(N, N):- !.
close_numbers(N, M):-
    N <= M + 1,
    N >= M - 1.
```

210

3.

```
near_miss(Word, NearWord):-
    word(NearWord),
    name(Word, Lword),
    name(NearWord, LNearWord),
    length(Word, LenWord),
    length(NearWord, LenNearWord),
    close_numbers(LenWord, LenNearWord),
    same_first(LWord, LNearWord),
    Half is LenWord // 2,
    same_chars(Word, NearWord, SameChars),
    SameChars > Half.
```

Exercises 8

Change all occurrences of **getchar** to **getlc** and define as follows:

```
getlc(C):-
    get0(C1),
    convert_lc(C1,C).
convert_lc(C1,C):-
    (C1 >= 65),
    (C1 =< 90),
    C is (C1 + 32),!.
convert_lc(C,C).
```

Exercises 9

1.

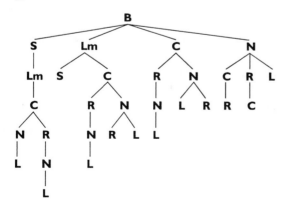

2.   B, S, Lm, C, N, L, R

3.   B, S, Lm, C, R

4.

```
depth_first(Start, Goal, Visited, [Start|Path]):-
   next_node(Start, Next_node, Visited),
   write(Visited),nl,
   depth_first(Next_node, Goal, [Next_node|Visited],
Path).
```

Exercises 10

3.   This is a slightly more comprehensive solution than has been asked for that does a certain amount of type checking.

```
go :-
   write('SQL> '),
   read_word_list(Wlist),
   !,
   nl,
   query(Wlist,[],Plist),
   !,
   validate_query(Plist),
   !,
   do_query(Plist).
query(S0,S,q(Sel,F,Where)):-
   select(S0,S1,Sel),
   from(S1,S2,F),
   where(S2,S,Where),!.
query(_,_,_):-
   nl,
   write('ERROR - could not understand query'),nl,
   fail.
select([select|S0],S,select(Names)):-
   colnames(S0,S,Names).
colnames(S0,S,[Name]):-
   colname(S0,S,Name).
colnames(S0,S,[Name|Names]):-
   colname(S0,S1,Name),
   colnames(S1,S,Names).
from([from|S0],S1,table(T)):-
   tablename(S0,S1,T),!.
```

```
where([],[],where([])):-!. /* no where clause in query */
where([where|S0],S1,where(Name,Op,Value)):-
    colname(S0,S2,Name),
    parse_operator(S2,S3,Op),
    value(S3,S1,Value).
validate_query(q(select(Colnames),table(Tname),_)):-
    validate_columns(Tname,Colnames).
validate_columns(_,[]):-!.
validate_columns(Tname,[Colname|Rest]):-
    data_dictionary(Tname,Colname,_,_,_),
    !,
    validate_columns(Tname,Rest).
do_query(q(select(Colnames),table(Tname),Where)):-
    get_col_nums(Tname,Colnames,Colnums),
    heading(Tname,Colnums),
    init_count,
    table(Tname,Rec),
    check_where(Where,Tname,Rec),
    output_view(Rec,Tname,Colnums),
    update_count,
    nl,
    fail.
do_query(_):-
    count(N),
    nl,
    write(N),
    write(' Rows selected'),nl.
heading(Tname,Colnums):-
    heading1(Tname,Colnums),nl,
    heading2(Tname,Colnums),nl.
heading1(_,[]):-!.
heading1(Tname,[H|T]):-
    data_dictionary(Tname,Colname,H,_,Len),
    !,
    pad_write(Colname,Len),
    heading1(Tname,T).
 heading2(_,[]):-!.
heading2(Tname,[H|T]):-
    write('+'),
    data_dictionary(Tname,_,H,_,Len),
    !,
```

213

```
            char_repeat('-',Len),
            heading2(Tname,T).
    init_count:-
            retract(count(_)),fail.
    init_count:-
            assertz(count(0)).
    update_count:-
            retract(count(Count)),
            Count1 is Count + 1,
            assertz(count(Count1)).
    check_where(where([]),_,_):-!. /* no where to check */
    check_where(where(Colname,Op,Value),Tname,Rec):-
            data_dictionary(Tname,Colname,Colnum,Type,_),
            !,
            valid_where(Type,Op),
            !,
            find_value(Colnum,1,Rec,V),
            apply_condition(V,Op,Value).
    valid_where(int,=):-!.
    valid_where(float,=):-!.
    valid_where(char,=):-!.
    valid_where(int,>):-!.
    valid_where(float,>):-!.
    valid_where(char,>):-!.
    valid_where(int,<):-!.
    valid_where(float,<):-!.
    valid_where(char,<):-!.
    valid_where(Type,Op):-
            nl,write('ERROR - cannot use operator '),
            write(Op),
            write(' with type '),
            write(Type),nl,
            fail.
    find_value(Colnum,Colnum,[V|_],V):-!.
    find_value(Colnum,N,[_|RestV],V):-
            M is N + 1,
            find_value(Colnum,M,RestV,V).
    apply_condition(V,=,V):-!.
    apply_condition(V,>,V1):- V @> V1.
    apply_condition(V,<,V1):- V @< V1.
     output_view(_,_,[]):-!.
```

```prolog
output_view(Rec,Tname,[Fieldno|Rest]):-
    data_dictionary(Tname,_,Fieldno,_,Len),
    !,
    getnth(Fieldno,Rec,Value),
    pad_write(Value,Len),
    output_view(Rec,Tname,Rest).
get_col_nums(_,[],[]):-!.
get_col_nums(Tname,[Col|Colrest],[Num|Numrest]):-
    data_dictionary(Tname,Col,Num,_,_),
    !,
    get_col_nums(Tname,Colrest,Numrest).
pad_write(Value,L):-
    name(Value,List),
    length(List,Len),
    L >= Len,
    !,
    write(' '),
    Pad is L - Len,
    write(Value),
    tab(Pad).
pad_write(Value,L):- /* truncate Value to length L */
    write(' '),
    name(Value,List),
    firstn(L,List,Nlist),
    name(Vtrunc,Nlist),
    write(Vtrunc).
colname([Colname|S],S,Colname):-
    data_dictionary(_,Colname,_,_,_),!.
tablename([Tname|S],S,Tname):-
    data_dictionary(Tname,_,_,_,_).
parse_operator([Op|S],S,Op):-
    operator(Op),!.
operator(=).
operator(>).
operator(<).
value([V|S],S,V). /* value is just the next element of
the list */
data_dictionary(emp,empno,1,int,4).
data_dictionary(emp,ename,2,char,10).
data_dictionary(emp,job,3,char,10).
data_dictionary(emp,mgr,4,int,4).
```

```
data_dictionary(emp,sal,5,float,7).
data_dictionary(emp,department,6,char,10).
/*
Now the table contents, this is how we represent the
contents of a user table.
*/
table(emp,[7658,chan,analyst,7566,3450.0,research]).
table(emp,[7782,clark,manager,7566,2572.0,accounting]).
table(emp,[7839,king,president,7566,5500.0,operations]).
table(emp,[7934,miller,clerk,7566,920.0,research]).
table(emp,[7999,brown,clerk,7566,800.0,accounting]).
table(emp,[7876,adams,clerk,7566,920.0,research]).
table(emp,[7369,smith,clerk,7566,929.0,sales]).
table(emp,[7566,jones,manager,7566,3123.0,research]).
table(emp,[7788,scott,analyst,7566,3759.0,sales]).
table(emp,[7902,ford,analyst,7566,3450.0,research]).
table(emp,[7657,mason,analyst,7566,3910.0,accounting]).
table(emp,[7659,fox,analyst,7566,3335.0,research]).
table(emp,[7499,allan,salesman,7566,1600.0,sales]).
table(emp,[7521,ward,salesman,7566,1312.0,sales]).
```

Exercises 13

```
rule company backward
    if query 'What company do you like? (students/young/
    posh/mixed) '
            receives_answer X
        & prolog(X=Y)
    then company(Y).
rule music backward
    if query 'What music do you like? (rock/irish/
    juke_box/none) '
            receives_answer X
        & prolog(X=Y)
    then music(Y).
rule drinks backward
    if query 'What do you like to drink? (real_ale/beer/
    spirits/guinness/anything) '
            receives_answer X
        & prolog(X=Y)
    then drinks(Y).
rule affords backward
```

216

```
    if query 'What can you afford? (expensive/moderate/
    cheap) '
            receives_answer X
        & prolog(X=Y)
    then affords(Y).
rule dog_and_trumpet backward
    if deduce music(rock)
        & deduce drinks(real_ale)
        & deduce affords(expensive)
    then recommended_pub(dog_and_trumpet).
rule union_bar backward
    if deduce affords(cheap)
        & deduce company(young)
    then recommended_pub(union_bar).
 rule eight_bells backward
    if deduce music(irish)
        & deduce company(mixed)
        & deduce drinks(guinness)
    then recommended_pub(eight_bells).
rule silver_sword backward
    if deduce music(live)
        & deduce company(young)
        & drinks(anything)
    then recommended_pub(silver_sword).
rule de_vere backward
    if deduce music(none)
        & deduce company(posh)
        & drinks(spirits)
        & affords(expensive)
    then recommended_pub(de_vere).
```

Index

Low-cost Prolog++ compiler offer from Logic Programming Associates

Congratulations! As the owner of Mastering Prolog by Rob Lucas, you are entitled to a special offer on Prolog++ compilers from Logic Programming Associates, one of the world's leading suppliers of Prolog-based development tools.

Available in both Macintosh and Windows 3.1 versions, Prolog++ enables programmers to define object taxonomies and manipulate them with Prolog rules – a powerful and elegant combination of object-oriented and logic programming technologies.

Key features of Prolog++ include

- Dynamic objects with attributes, functions and methods
- Class hierarchies with single and multiple inheritance
- Private and local methods that can be easily edited
- Full access to the underlying Prolog
- An interactive development environment, with object browsers and inspectors

System requirements
Microsoft Windows 3.1 with a minimum of 6Mb of RAM
Macintosh System 7 with a minimum of 6Mb of RAM

PRIORITY ORDER

I would like to order the following copies of the Entry Level Prolog++compiler for
[delete as appropriate]

No.		Cost
_____Windows 3.1 @ £34.95 (UK) / $57.95 (other countries)		_____
_____Macintosh @ £34.95 (UK) / $57.95 (other countries)		_____
Please add VAT @ 17.5% for orders from the UK and EU countries		_____
Postage & packing £5.00/$8.00 per copy		_____
	Total	_____

Name   Job title

Organization

Address

                                                  Post code

Tel.:   Fax:

Visa ☐   Mastercard ☐   Cheque ☐   [cheques payable to Logic Programming Associates Ltd.]

Cardholder's name

Address

Card number   Expiry date

Signature

Logic Programming Associates Ltd
Studio 4, RVPB, Trinity Road, London SW18 3SX, UK
Tel: 0181 871 2016 (Int.: +44 181 871 2016)
Fax: 0181 874 0449 (Int.: +44 181 874 0449)
Email: lpa@cix.compulink.co.uk   World Wide Web Page: http://www.lpa.co.uk